D1299855

ISTITUTO NAZIONALE
DI STUDI SUL RINASCIMENTO

QUADERNI DI
«RINASCIMENTO»
·44·

ISTITUTO
NAZIONALE
DI STUDI
SUL
RINASCIMENTO

QUADERNI DI
«RINASCIMENTO»
• 44 •

JAMES HANKINS – ADA PALMER

The Recovery of Ancient Philosophy in the Renaissance: A Brief Guide

Leo S. Olschki Editore
MMVIII

Published with a contribution from the Department of History,
Harvard University

ISBN 978 88 222 5769 7

CONTENTS

— V —

CONTENTS

INTRODUCTION

Historians of philosophy have long recognized that the defining cultural project of the Renaissance period – bringing back to life the arts and literature of the lost Greco-Roman world – had an enormous impact on the study of philosophy in the West. It changed fundamentally what philosophers studied and how they studied. At the beginning of the period, commonly dated to around the mid-fourteenth century, philosophical activity was mostly confined to university arts and theology faculties and the *studia* of religious orders. The works of Aristotle were the center of the curriculum, and the primary modes of philosophical inquiry were commentary and disputation. By the end of the Renaissance, this situation had changed radically. While Aristotle remained a key author in universities well into the century of Descartes, Hobbes, Spinoza and Leibniz, his dominance was being successfully challenged, not only by the "new philosophies", but also by vigorous revivals of Platonism, Stoicism, Epicureanism and Skepticism. In one field after another his authority was undermined: first in moral philosophy by Petrarch and the humanists, then in logic by the Ramists, finally in the inmost citadel of Aristotelianism, physics and natural philosophy. Inside and outside the universities scholastic method was being supplemented and in part replaced by new, more historically-aware disciplines of textual scholarship that had been popularized by the humanist movement. Thanks in part to the flood of new texts made readily available by the printing press, philosophers were less inclined to regard Aristotle as an ideal teacher of timeless truths and more inclined to see him as a moment in the evolution of ancient philosophical thought. In advanced circles Aristotle was even seen as an establishment figure who had successfully carried off a *damnatio memoriae* of his predecessors – Presocratics and ancient theologians – predecessors whose philosophies were seen by men such as Bruno, Galileo, and Campanella as more profound, more "Mosaic", and therefore more compatible with Christian truth than the vulgar Aristotelianism that had imposed itself on the schools in the Middle Ages. Many Renaissance scholars were determined to bring an end to the suppression of alternative philosophies, whether ancient or modern.[1]

It is, to be sure, wrong to think that Aristotle's role as the backbone of the curriculum in arts faculties meant that medieval thinkers had no knowledge of other ancient philosophical traditions. Although they had limited access to Plato's own dialogues,[2] scholastic thinkers, especially theologians, were familiar with the *Denkwelt* of Middle and Neo-Platonism via Pseudo-Dionysius the Areopagite, Proclus' *Elements of Theology*, Arab philosophers such as Algazel and Avicenna, as well as ancient Latin accounts of Platonism in authors like Cicero, Seneca, Apuleius, Augustine and Boethius.[3] The doctrines of the Stoics, especially their moral teachings, were also known via indirect sources.[4] Academic skepticism was accessible through Cicero and Augustine's *Contra Academicos*. The names and a few key doctrines of the Pre-Socratics and of Socrates himself could be found in Aristotle's reports of their teachings.[5] Yet it remains true that medieval scholastic commentary on ancient philosophy was almost always focused on a handful of Aristotelian texts, and the vast majority of the ancient philosophical texts that survive today, aside from those of Aristotle, were unknown or unavailable. And almost all the ancient pagan philosophical texts known today, always excepting those of Aristotle, were rediscovered, translated, studied and printed in the Renaissance. The present *Guide* is intended in part to document this vast movement to recover and assimilate the pagan philosophy of the Greco-Roman world.

The recovery of ancient philosophy in the Renaissance is not only a movement of great interest in its own right. It is also a subject of great practical importance to all scholars concerned with the role of ancient philosophical thought in the theology, philosophy, political theory, literature and arts of the Renaissance and early modern period. It is often a question highly relevant to the interpretation of an author or an artist whether or not that person could have known a particular ancient philosopher at a particular time, in what languages that philosopher's work might have been available, and what commentaries were available to guide the study of the philosopher's work. To provide such detailed information about all the ancient writers, pagan and Christian,

---

[1] See the Introduction and Conclusion in HANKINS 2007b.

[2] HANKINS 1990. The only Platonic text for which there is a medieval commentary tradition is the *Timaeus*, the first third of which was translated and commented on by Calcidius; see PLATO, below.

[3] HANKINS 2003-04, 2:7-26; for the Latin tradition of Platonism see GERSH 1986.

[4] VERBEKE 1983.

[5] LAARMANN 1995.

is of course the province of the *Catalogus Translationum et Commentariorum*, founded in 1945 by Paul Oskar Kristeller, which has now published eight volumes covering more than 80 ancient authors.[6] Yet the progress of this vital work remains slow and the information most relevant to the student of Renaissance and early modern philosophy is not easily retrievable. Where the *CTC* provides coverage of an author, precise and accurate data is available, and the authors of this *Guide* have made grateful use of it. But for the great majority of authors there is as yet no *CTC* article, and no one place that a student can turn to extract quickly the most vital data concerning the reception of an ancient philosophical author.

This purpose of this *Guide* is far more modest that that of the *CTC*. It aims to show at what point the major texts and sources of ancient pagan philosophy became available in Renaissance Europe (1350-1600) and which translators and commentators shaped their initial reception. Included in principle are the dates of first printing and, in the case of works originally in Greek, the dates when they were first translated into Latin. Where possible, mention is made of the most important commentaries and the earliest vernacular translations, though in the current state of bibliographical research complete and reliable information is not always available on these subjects. Given space limitations it has also not been possible to treat testimonia and fragments in detail, especially those found in the Greek and Latin Church Fathers. Where possible, studies that survey the manuscript transmission of an author and manuscript commentaries on an author have been cited, but the reader should be aware that for many authors, including central figures such as Cicero, comprehensive studies of the manuscript tradition are still lacking in the modern scholarly literature.

Names printed in small caps indicate authors or traditions treated in separate entries elsewhere in the *Guide*. Unless otherwise specified, information about printed editions comes from Flodr 1973 and Risse 1998, supplemented by electronic catalogs such as the *Incunabula Short-Title Catalogue* (British Library), WorldCat (Online Computer Library Center) and the Karlsruhe Virtueller Katalog (Universität Karlsruhe).

This *Guide* was originally intended to stand as an appendix in the *Cambridge Companion to Renaissance Philosophy*, edited by James Hankins (2007). It soon grew far too large to be included in that volume, and we are most grateful to Michele Ciliberto, Presidente of the Istituto Nazionale di Studi sul Rinascimento, who kindly offered to give it a suitable home in the "Quaderni

---

[6] *CTC* (see ABBREVIATIONS).

di Rinascimento". We are also grateful to Gerard J. Boter, Virginia Brown, Gian Mario Cao, Brian P. Copenhaver, Julia Haig Gaisser, Jill Kraye and Marianne Pade for information and assistance of various kinds.

Florence, November 2007

JAMES HANKINS and ADA PALMER

I

PRESOCRATICS AND SOPHISTS

The term "Presocratic" refers to all Greek philosophy before the lifetime of Socrates (b. 469 BC) and includes early natural philosophers of the Italian and Ionian schools like Thales, Anaximander, Heraclitus, Parmenides, Anaxagoras, Zeno of Elea, Democritus and Pythagoras as well as the sophists of the fifth century BC. Most of what the Renaissance knew about Presocratic natural philosophy derived from ARISTOTLE'S summaries of their views in his own works, particularly the *Physics*, *Metaphysics* and *De caelo*, from COMMENTATORS on Aristotle, from CICERO, or from DIOGENES LAERTIUS' *Lives of the Philosophers* (see BIOGRAPHY). Other testimonia could be found in PLATO, PLUTARCH'S *Moralia*, the doxographic writers (see DOXOGRAPHIES AND ANTHOLOGIES), in the Greek Church Fathers and in medical writings, especially Galen and the Hippocratic corpus. The first printed collection of Presocratic fragments was *Poesis philosophica, vel saltem reliquiae poesis philosophicae Empedoclis, Parmenidis, Xenophanis, Cleanthis, Timonis, Epicharmi; adiuncta sunt Orphei illius carmina qui a suis appellatus fuit ὁ θεολόγος; item, Heracliti et Democriti loci quidam et eorum epistolae*, published by Henri II Estienne (Stephanus) with the help of Joseph Scaliger in 1573; this included quotations extracted from Greek, patristic and Byzantine sources (Kraye 2003, 340). For Renaissance fragment collections of Pythagoras, see NEOPYTHAGOREANS.

The work of the sophists, whose philosophical contribution was primarily in the realm of epistemology and ethics, was known chiefly through testimonia in PLATO and ARISTOTLE and their commentators, Xenophon (see SOCRATES), CICERO, Quintilian, PLUTARCH'S *Moralia*, DIOGENES LAERTIUS, SEXTUS EMPIRICUS, and Philostratus' *Lives of the Sophists* (see BIOGRAPHY), as well as scattered passages in Dionysius of Halicarnassus, Athenaeus and the Greek Church Fathers. In the Renaissance, neither the Presocratic natural philosophers nor the sophists were understood to constitute distinct phases of Greek philosophical history, and the Renaissance conception of the sophist usually reflected the negative stereotypes in Plato (Trinkaus 1983).

II

SOCRATES

Socrates (469-399 BC) was claimed by PLATONISTS, ARISTOTELIANS, CYNICS, STOICS and SKEPTICS alike as a model for their traditions of philosophical life. He left no writings, but is mentioned by dozens of classical sources (Ferguson 1970). The most important are the dialogues of PLATO, though no Renaissance scholar addressed seriously the issue of distinguishing Plato's Socrates from the historical Socrates. Other major sources included Xenophon, who like Plato was a disciple of Socrates and who discussed him in his *Apologia, Memorabilia, Oeconomicus* and *Symposium*; DIOGENES LAERTIUS; Aristophanes, who satirized Socrates in *The Clouds, The Wasps, The Birds* and *The Frogs*; APULEIUS' *On Socrates' God*; and Maximus of Tyre. ARISTOTLE too discusses Socrates' views, especially in the *Metaphysics, Nicomachean Ethics* and *Magna Moralia*. Ancient testimonia to Socrates' life and teaching in CICERO, SENECA, DIO CHRYSOSTOM (especially discourses 54 and 55), Lucian, PLUTARCH (especially the *De genio Socratis* in *Moralia* 575a-598e), and APULEIUS were particularly well known in the Renaissance. The engagement of the Greek Fathers with Socrates (Frede 2006) became better known after a new wave of patristic translations that began with the Council of Florence in 1438-39 (Gentile 1997).

Xenophon's *Apology* was translated into Latin before 1407 by the humanist Leonardo Bruni and this translation circulated widely in manuscript (Hankins 1997). It was first printed in Milan in 1467 and was frequently reprinted. The *Memorabilia* was translated into Latin in 1442 by Cardinal Bessarion, though the version was not printed until 1521. Raffaele Maffei (called Raphael Volterranus) turned the *Oeconomicus* into Latin in an edition first printed in 1506 in Rome. The *Symposium* was the latest to become known in Latin: it was translated in 1545 by Johannes Ribittus (Jean Ribit) and in 1546 by the Frankfurt humanist Janus Cornarius (Johann Haynpul); the latter's rendering was first printed by Oporinus in Basel in 1548. The *Symposium* and *Oeconomicus* were first printed in Greek in 1516, the *Apologia Socratis* in 1520 and the *Memorabilia* in 1529. Xenophon's Socratic works began to be translated into vernacular languages in the 1520s and 30s, beginning with the popular *Oeconomicus*. Major commentaries on Xenophon were composed by Joachim Camerarius (1543) and Franciscus Portus (1586), while Henri Estienne (Stephanus) published an important critical *Opera omnia* with improved Latin translations and notes in 1561 (Marsh 1992).

A translation of the *Dialexeis* of Maximus of Tyre was not made until the 1490s, nor published until 1517 (tr. Cosimus Paccius), but several manuscripts of the Greek text circulated and were read in Florence and Venice between 1420 and 1490 (Maximus of Tyre 1997; Trapp 1997-98); the *editio princeps* was printed by Henricus II Stephanus in 1557. A translation and commentary on Maximus' *Dialexeis* by Daniel Heinsius was published in 1607. Parts of Aristophanes were translated into Latin as early as the 1420s and 1430s, though nothing from the comedies mentioning Socrates (Brenta 1993); the first Greek edition of the plays was printed by Aldus Manutius in Venice in 1498, and the first complete Latin translation was undertaken by Andreas Divus in an edition first printed in Venice in 1538; an Italian translation by Bartolomeo and Pietro Rositini followed in 1545. The pseudonymous letters of Socrates, Antisthenes and the Socratics were not published until 1637.

Other important sources for the Renaissance image of Socrates were Giannozzo Manetti's *Life of Socrates*, written in the 1440s and first printed in 1502, and various passages in the works of Marsilio Ficino (Manetti 2003; Hankins 2007a). Agostino Nifo composed an *Apologia Socratis et Aristotelis* (1526), Girolamo Cardano wrote an oration *De Socratis studio* (Cardano 1663, 1:151-58) and Daniel Heinsius composed an oration on the life and mores of Socrates that was published in 1612.

III

THE CYNICS AND THE *TABLET OF CEBES*

Among the philosophers who traced their lineage back to Socrates were the Cynics, an important ancient philosophical subculture which produced a large body of writings, very few of which survive (Paquet 1988). The Renaissance knew the Cynics primarily through CICERO, SENECA, DIO CHRYSOSTOM, DIOGENES LAERTIUS, Lucian, EPICTETUS, PLUTARCH, JULIAN THE APOSTATE, Stobaeus (see DOXOGRAPHIES AND ANTHOLOGIES) and a scattering of patristic sources, plus the pseudonymous letters attributed to the two chief philosophers of the sect, Diogenes the Cynic and Crates of Thebes.

The letters of Pseudo-Diogenes the Cynic were translated by Francesco Griffolini of Arezzo between 1458 and 1464 (with two dedications to Pius II) and were first printed in Nuremberg around 1475; the *editio princeps* of part of the corpus was printed by Aldus in his *Epistolarum graecarum collectio* of 1499. There were at least fourteen editions in all languages between 1475 and 1609. The pseudonymous letters attributed to Crates of Thebes, the Cynic philosopher, were translated first by Athanasius of Constantinople and published in 1474/78; the first Greek text was printed in the aforementioned Aldine collection of 1499. The Pseudo-Crates letters, in a new translation by Bartolomaeus Coloniensis, were printed in 1501, together with the Pseudo-Diogenes letters, and the same Bartolomeus added an account of the sect when his translation was reprinted in 1512.[1] In 1512 Rudolphus Agricola of Wasserburg (Bavaria) published in Kráków the collection of Pseudo-Crates letters and, when the collection was reprinted in 1518, added a life of Crates and a poem "on the misery of human life".[2] An early study of Diogenes the

---

[1] *Diogenis Cynici secta [authore Bartolomeo Coloniense latine]. Insignia Diogenis. Breviores epistolae Diogenis. Cratis philosophi cynici epistolae*, Wittenberg 1508; reprinted Erfort 1510, 1512 (RISSE 1998, 1:28).

[2] *Cratis Thebani Cynici philosophi epistole aureis sententiis referte theologie consentanee*, Kráków 1512; [...] *adiectis quibusdam praeclaris philosophorum sententiis et Cratis Cynici vita, per Rudolphum Agricolam iuniorem cum carmine eiusdem de miseria vitae humanae*, Kráków 1518 (RISSE 1998, 1:32, 40).

Cynic was written by Anthony Stafford in 1615.[3] A French translation of the Pseudo-Diogenes letters was made by Loys Du Puys and published in 1546 and 1549.

In addition to the pseudonymous letters of Diogenes and Crates, Lucian in his essays (*editio princeps* 1496) gives a portrait of the Cynic Demonax, otherwise unknown. A discussion of the Renaissance phase in the reception of the Cynics can be found in Matton 1996 and Cutler 2006, chapter 2; for a discussion of Cynic influence on Renaissance literature from Erasmus to Montaigne, see Clément 2005, which also contains an edition of Du Puys' French translation of pseudo-Diogenes. See also DIO CHRYSOSTOM.

Cebes of Thebes is mentioned in Plato's *Crito* and *Phaedo* as among the disciples of Socrates present during his last days, and Diogenes Laertius (3.125) attributed three works to him, including the *Pinax* (or *Tabula* in Latin). Modern scholars generally date the popular work that has been passed down with the title *The Tablet of Cebes* to the first century BC, and discern in it elements of Cynicism, Stoicism and Platonism. But in the Renaissance the text was universally ascribed to Cebes of Thebes, the interlocuter of Plato's dialogues, and was generally seen as broadly Platonic in inspiration, partly because it was known that Cebes studied with Philolaus, one of Ficino's "ancient theologians". The text itself gives an allegorical-moral reading of a tablet said to have been designed by a follower of Pythagoras and Parmenides. It was frequently handed down with the Epictetus' *Enchiridion*, not because of any perceived doctrinal associations with Stoicism but because both were considered guides to moral education.

Cebes' Tablet was among the most popular texts of the Renaissance, printed 47 times before 1600 in a variety of languages. The first Greek edition was printed in Florence in 1496, and the first Latin translation, made by Lodovico Odassi, appeared in 1497. It was reprinted many times. Other Latin translations were made by Theodoricus Adamaeus (1539), Justus Velsius (1557) and Hieronymus Wolf (1595/96). The work also appeared in English (Sir Francis Poyntz, 1530; J. Healey, 1536), French (G. Tory de Bourges, 1529; Gilles Corrozet, 1543), Spanish ("el Doctor Poblacion", 1532; Ambrosio de Morales, 1586), Italian (F. A. Coccio, 1538), Dutch (M. A. Gilles, 1564) and Polish (1581). Commentaries were composed by Joannes Camers (1524) and Justus Velsius (1551).

---

[3] *Heavenly dogge: or the life and death of that great Cynicke Diogenes*, London 1615 (RISSE 1998, 7:75).

2

IV

PLATO, EARLY PLATONISM, AND COMMENTATORS ON PLATO

A. PLATO

The dialogues of Plato (ca. 427-347 BC) were not entirely neglected in the middle ages, but medieval readers had access only to the parts of the *Timaeus* translated by CALCIDIUS and CICERO, plus opaquely literal versions of the *Meno* and *Phaedo* made in Sicily during the twelfth century by Henricus Aristippus and the portion of the *Parmenides* contained in PROCLUS' commentary on that text, which was translated about 1280 by the Dominican William of Moerbeke, working for Thomas Aquinas. Much was also known indirectly about Plato via the Latin philosophical tradition; especially informative were the works of CICERO, APULEIUS, MACROBIUS and Augustine. The Latin ARISTOTLE and his Arabic commentators were also important for the medieval knowledge of Plato. But the only text of Plato regularly commented on (and mostly before the 1230s) was the *Timaeus* in CALCIDIUS' partial version, to 53C (Hankins 1990, 2003-04). Much of the medieval study of the *Timaeus* took place in Northern France in the schools of Chartres and Paris.

In the later fourteenth century the study of CALCIDIUS and his Chartrian commentators was revived and continued to the middle of the fifteenth century. But by far the most important achievement of humanist philosophical scholarship in the fifteenth century was the gradual recovery and translation of the Platonic corpus into Latin. Leonardo Bruni, Uberto Decembrio and Cencio de' Rustici, all pupils of the émigré Greek Manuel Chrysoloras (d. 1415), translated among them some ten dialogues, including the *Gorgias* (1409), *Crito* (1404/9), *Phaedo* (1405), *Apology* (1404/9) and *Republic* (ca. 1402), part of the *Phaedrus* (1424), and a speech from the *Symposium* (1435). In the following generation the *Republic* was translated twice more, by Uberto Decembrio's son Pier Candido (late 1430s) and by the Sicilian Antonio Cassarino (1440s). The Milanese humanist Francesco Filelfo translated the *Euthyphro* and some of the *Letters* in the 1430s, while in Rome the papal secretary Rinuccio Aretino rendered the *Crito*, *Euthyphro* and the pseudo-Platonic *Axiochus* (all before 1440). George of Trebizond, a humanist and papal secretary from Venetian Crete, turned the *Laws* (1450/51) and *Parmenides* (1458/59) into Latin. In Florence, Lorenzo Lippi da Colle, a neo-Latin poet and *protégé* of Piero de' Medici, translated the *Ion* (1464-69). The translation activity of the humanists culminated in the work of Marsilio Ficino, who in 1484 published the first complete Latin version of Plato's works. So while in 1400 the Latin world possessed only two complete and two partial versions of the Platonic dialogues and a developed commentary tradition only on the *Timaeus*, by the end of the fifteenth century it had available in Latin all thirty-six dialogues of the Thrasyllan canon and a large and sophisticated body of ancient and modern commentaries and other aids to the study of Plato's texts (Hankins 1990).

The progress of Platonic studies continued in the sixteenth century. Ficino's *Platonis opera* in Latin was reprinted 28 times, often in one of three revised versions (1532, 1557 and 1592), made respectively by Simon Grynaeus, Marcus Hopper and Etienne Tremblay. There were also two fresh Latin versions of the complete works, those of Janus Cornarius (1561) and Jean de Serre or Serranus (1578), printed with Stephanus' Greek text. The *editio princeps* of the Platonic corpus in Greek, edited by Marcus Musurus, was published by Aldus in 1513. It was followed by the major recensions of Simon Grynaeus (1534), Marcus Hopper (1556) and Henri II Estienne or Stephanus (1578). The latter edition remained in use until the early nineteenth century, and its pagination still provides the standard reference system for Plato's works. The trickle of vernacular translations of Plato that began in the fifteenth century turned into a flood in the sixteenth, though the first complete edition of Plato's works in a vernacular language was Dardi Bembo's Italian version published in 1601 (Hankins 1990).

The principal philosophical commentator on Plato in the Renaissance was Ficino, who wrote major commentaries on the *Timaeus*, *Philebus*, *Parmenides*, *Phaedrus*, *Sophist* and the passage on the "Platonic Number" in *Republic VIII*, as well as his famous commentary on the *Symposium* (1467/69), written in the form of a series of after-dinner speeches. This work, known as *The Banquet* or *De amore*, was reprinted many times and was a major influence on the Renaissance theory of love. Ficino also wrote shorter *argumenta* to all of the dialogues that did not receive full commentaries (including arguments for each book of the *Republic* and *Laws*) which were first printed with Ficino's commentaries in 1484, the *editio princeps*, again with *corrigenda* in 1491, and with many later printings of Ficino's translation. Ficino's major commentaries were printed in 1496 in expanded form, but without the *argumenta*. It should be noted that Ficino expected his commentaries and translations of the dialogues to be read together with his *Platonic Theology on the Immortality of the Soul* in eighteen books, first published in 1482. Ficino's commentaries were also printed, together with the *Theology*, in the editions of Ficino's own *Opera omnia* of 1561, 1576 and 1641 (Hankins 1990).

In addition to Ficino's commentaries, Cardinal Bessarion's *In calumniatorem Platonis* (1469 and later editions) provided a kind of introduction to Plato from a Neoplatonic perspective. A few other philosophical commentaries were written on Plato in the sixteenth century, but none dealt comprehensively with the dialogues apart from the extensive materials compiled by Henri Estienne and Jean de Serre accompanying the Stephanus edition of 1578. These offered an interpretation of Plato that attempted to strip his texts of "les gloses des Platoniciens", meaning the Neoplatonists, and to return to the historical Plato, who was considered to be harmonious with Aristotle and, used with prudence, compatible with Christianity (Tigerstedt 1974, 39-41). The Stephanus-de Serre edition was regarded as a work of Calvinist scholarship and tended to be most popular in Protestant lands. A number of individual dialogues also received philosophical commentaries, of which the most important were Sebastian Fox Morzillo's commentaries on the *Timaeus* (1554), *Republic* (1556) and *Phaedo* (1556), Petrus Ramus' commentary on the *Epistulae* (1549), and Louis Le Roy's commentary in French on the *Republic* (1552). For sixteenth-century study of the *Timaeus* see Neschke-Hentschke 2000; Hankins 2003-04 and 2005; for Plato's political thought in the Renaissance see Neschke-Hentschke 1995-2003.

B. Pseudo-Plato

In the Renaissance Pseudo-Plato was often as well known as Plato himself, and the most popular "Platonic" dialogue of the Renaissance may well have been the *Axiochus*, put into Latin by fourteen separate translators (earliest 1426/31 by Rinuccio Aretino) and widely circulated in dozens of printed editions; it was the only work attributed to Plato translated into English during the Renaissance (1592). In the fifteenth century the *Letters* were translated by Leonardo Bruni (1427/34) and circulated widely in manuscript; George of Trebizond added the *Epinomis* to his version of the *Laws* (1450/51); the *Halcyon* was translated as early as the 1430s by Agostino Dati. Ficino translated the *Axiochus* and the *Definitions*, attributing them to Xenocrates and Speusippus respectively. Both were translated around 1464 but only published in 1497. The standard collection of six *spuria* (*Definitions*, *On Justice*, *On Virtue*, *Demodocus*, *Sisyphus*, *Eryxias*) was not included in Latin translations of Plato's complete works until Cornarius added them to his *Opera omnia* of 1561, though individual items had circulated earlier. De Serre also provided versions of the spurious works in his 1578 translation and the Greek texts of the *spuria* were included in all editions of the Greek *Opera omnia* (Hankins 1990).

Doubts had been entertained about the authenticity of works in the canon as early as the 1420s, when Bruni rejected two letters of Plato on internal grounds. Ficino's canon of Plato was based on Thrasyllus and the list of Plato's works in DIOGENES LAERTIUS as well as on the Greek manuscript tradition of Plato, but like Bruni he rejected *Letter XIII* and like many modern scholars considered the *Clitopho* spurious on internal grounds. Diogenes Laertius and Ficino's Greek codices rejected the six *spuria*, but the *On Justice* and *On Virtue* were given to Plato in manuscripts of Stobaeus; Conrad Gesner rejected the attribution when he added them to his translation of Stobaeus in 1543. *Letter XIII*, marked as spurious, was added back to the collection of Plato's works by Cornarius and Serranus (Hankins 1990).

C. OLD ACADEMY AND MIDDLE PLATONISM

The concepts of the Old Academy and the Skeptical Academy were known and used in the Renaissance thanks to CICERO and SEXTUS EMPIRICUS, but the term "Middle Platonism" is of recent coinage (though some prefer the term "Pre-Neoplatonism") and refers to the period of Platonic philosophy extending from the time of Antiochus of Ascalon (d. ca. 68 BC) to the time of PLOTINUS. It should be noted that Renaissance models of the history of Platonism are more complex and differ in emphasis, as for example in the works of Ficino (Allen 1998; Hankins 2006). The Hellenistic subdivisions of the Skeptical Academy into two or three Academies was known from SEXTUS EMPIRICUS' *Outlines of Pyrrhonism* (1.33).

The chief figures associated with the Old Academy, in addition to Plato himself, were Speusippus, Xenocrates, Polemon and Crates. The most important source on the last four figures in the Renaissance was DIOGENES LAERTIUS; it was on the basis of the lists of works in Diogenes that Ficino attributed the *Definitions* to Speusippus and the *Axiochus* to Xenocrates (see PSEUDO-PLATO). For the Skeptical Academy, which flourished from the mid-third to the mid-first century BC, see SKEPTICS.

Middle Platonism represented a reaction to skepticism and was marked by eclectic tendencies as well as a greater interest in systematic metaphysics, and it was deeply influenced by the NEOPYTHAGOREANS. The chief surviving philosophers from this period are PLUTARCH, ALCINOUS and APULEIUS. Other authors known in the Renaissance from testimonia included Antiochus (known chiefly from CICERO), Albinus, Atticus, Eudorus and Numenius. Galen was also deeply influenced by Middle Platonism (see DOXOGRAPHIES AND ANTHOLOGIES). Roman writers familiar with contemporary Greek philosophy such as CICERO, SENECA and Aulus Gellius or Christian authors like Tertullian, Hermias, Arnobius, Lactantius, Eusebius, CALCIDIUS and Augustine also discuss Middle Platonic themes and authors (Gersh 1986). The medical writer Galen, a pupil of Albinus, is another important source. On Gellius in the Renaissance see Baron 1968; on Galen see DOXOGRAPHIES AND ANTHOLOGIES.

1. *Plutarch*

Plutarch (b. after 45 AD, d. after 140 AD) was best known in the Renaissance for his *Lives*, but his *Moralia* were also read, studied and translated. The latter contain, in addition to many essays on moral topics, several more technical essays discussing Platonic themes and attacking Stoic and Epicurean philosophers. Translation activity on the *Moralia* began with a translation of the *De cohibenda ira* in 1373 by Simone Autumano. In the course of the fifteenth century some 32 of the 78 essays contained in the *Moralia* were translated by two dozen humanist translators, some several times. The most popular was *De educatione puerorum* in the translation by Guarino Veronese (ca. 1410). Most of these Latin versions circulated only in manuscript and usually as separate essays. The humanist translators concentrated on the essays principally concerned with moral philosophy and avoided the more technical pieces (Giustiniani 1979; Bevagni 1994). Ficino, however, used extensively the essays *De fato* and the *De animae procreatione in Timaeo* in his 1496 commentary on the *Timaeus* (Hankins 2003-04).

The complete Greek text of the *Moralia* was first printed in a 1509 Aldine edition entitled *Plutarchi opuscula LXXXXII*, based on a Venetian manuscript which had belonged to Cardinal Bessarion. The first complete Latin translation was published in 1526, which collected renderings of individual essays by Guillaume Budé, Erasmus, Willibald Pirckheimer, Poliziano, and other translators. A corrected edition of the Aldine Greek text was printed by Froben in Basel (1542), and a bilingual Latin and Greek edition appeared in 1570. Henri Estienne (Stephanus) printed a thirteen-volume bilingual Latin and Greek *Opera* of Plutarch in 1572 with the Latin translations of Gulielmus Xylander; this became the standard edition for early modern Europe.

There was a famous French translation made by Jacques Amyot in 1572; less well known is the Spanish version (1548) of Diego Gracián, a student of Vives. The first English version of the *Moralia* was that of Philemon Holland (1603). Individual essays continued to be translated and published separately; for example Louis Le Roy's French translation of the *De animae procreatione in Timaeo* was published in the 1552 and 1582 editions of his translation and commentary on Plato's *Timaeus*.

Four books of disputations illustrating the *Moralia*, written by Andreas Matthaeus Aquavivus, were published in 1609. For Pseudo-Plutarch's *On the Teachings of the Philosophers* (in *Moralia*, Book XI), see DOXOGRAPHIES AND ANTHOLOGIES.

2. *Alcinous*

Nothing is known of the Middle Platonic author Alcinous, the author of a *Handbook of Platonism* (*Didaskalicon*); the identification of him with another Middle Platonist, Albinus, first made by Jakob Freudenthal in 1879, is now regarded as dubious. Alcinous wrote in Greek and probably flourished in the second century AD. His *Handbook* was first translated into Latin before 1460 by Pietro Balbi, an associate of Bessarion and Nicholas of Cusa, and was printed in Rome in 1469 with a dedication to Bessarion as an addendum to an edition of the works of APULEIUS. Ficino translated the text before 1464 and circulated it among his associates before sending it to Aldus Manutius in Venice to print (1497), together with his other translations from ancient Platonists (Kristeller 1938). A third translation was produced by the French scholar Denys Lambin in 1567 together with a philological commentary. The Greek text was first printed as an appendix to the works of Apuleius at the Aldine press in Venice in 1521; another Greek edition was published in Paris in 1532; later editions of the Greek text were prepared by Arsenius Apostolides in 1535 and by Lambin in 1567 (Alcinous 1990). *Scholia* on the text were composed by Matthaeus Frigillanus which were published in Paris in 1562.

3. *Theon of Smyrna*

Theon of Smyrna (fl. ca. 110-140 AD) was the author of an extant work, *Aspects of Mathematics Useful for Reading Plato*. A translation was made by Ficino but was not published (Allen 1994); it survives in two manuscripts, the second copied by Lucas Holstenius. The text was not published until 1644, when it appeared with a Latin translation by Ismael Boulliau.

4. *Apuleius*

Apuleius (ca. 125-after 170 AD) wrote two important philosophical works in Latin, the *De deo Socratis*, a lecture on the nature of Socrates' guardian *daimon*, and *De Platone et eius dogmate*, a summary of Platonic doctrine. The *De mundo*, a Latin paraphrase of a pseudo-Aristotelian work written in Greek, and the *Asclepius*, a portion of the HERMETIC CORPUS surviving in Latin, were both passed down with the works of Apuleius and were often attributed to him as author (Goulet 1989-2005, 1:298-317). Apuleius in fact presents himself as the author of the *De mundo* ("following Aristotle and Theophrastus") but the survival of the Greek text showed some scholars already in the early fifteenth century that Apuleius' role had been closer to that of a translator (Kraye 2002). Via a different strand of the manuscript tradition a short treatise entitled *De interpretatione*, the oldest work on formal logic written in Latin, was also transmitted under Apuleius' name; it was known throughout the Middle Ages and was first printed in 1528. Apuleius also wrote an *Apologia*, an oration in self-defense against charges of magic, and the long novel *Metamorphoses*, his most celebrated work, which contains the Platonic tale of Cupid and Psyche (4.28-6.24). Apuleius was an important source for Western medieval Platonism (Gersh 1986) and his philosophical works circulated widely in manuscript (Klibansky and Regen 1993).

Apuleius' philosophical works were also known indirectly via Augustine. The latter presents a detailed refutation of *De deo Socratis* in *The City of God* books 8 and 9 and quotes from *De mundo*, which he attributes to Apuleius. He discusses the *Asclepius*, but does not attribute it to Apuleius. Apuleius' philosophical works probably survived because of their association with Augustine. Fragments of otherwise unknown works of Apuleius are preserved in the grammarians Priscian and Charisius and in Johannes Lydus. A list of spurious works attributed to Apuleius may be found in Munk Olsen 1982, 1:5-34.

Apuleius was first printed in Rome in 1469 in an edition prepared by Giovanni Andrea de' Bussi, a member of Bessarion's circle. It contained both the *De deo Socratis* and *De Platone et eius dogmate* as well as the *Asclepius* and the *De mundo*. A summary and some notes on the *Asclepius* were published by Jacques Lefèvre d'Etaples in 1505, and full commentary was published in 1590 by Hannibal Rosselius, a Franciscan theologian (Dannenfeldt 1960b). Kaspar Schoppe composed *Symbola critica* on Apuleius' philosophical works in 1605.[4]

---

[4] *Symbola critica in Lucii Apuleii philosophi platonici opera*, Strasbourg 1605 (RISSE 1998, 7:70).

D. COMMENTATORS

1. *Calcidius*

Calcidius or, less correctly, Chalcidius, was a Christian author of the fourth-century AD who translated the first part (to 53c) of the *Timaeus* and added a commentary drawing upon various Middle Platonic and Neoplatonic sources. It was the most important point of access to Plato's own writings for the Latin West in the Middle Ages and continued to be widely read and studied in the Renaissance. The text and commentary was the subject of several major sets of glosses in the twelfth century, including those of Bernard of Chartres and William of Conches, and these glosses, too, continued to be used by Renaissance readers. Of the 198 known manuscripts of Calcidius, about a quarter were copied or were documentably present in Italy during the Renaissance. From the fourteenth century there are two important glossators on Calcidius: an anonymous contemporary of Petrarch (the "1363 Commentator") and Antonius de Romagno, a humanist from Veneto. In the fifteenth century there are a number of glossed copies, one seemingly showing that the text was studied by a philosophy master at the University of Padua. Other annotators of Calcidius included Marsilio Ficino, his associate Pierleone da Spoleto and Giovanni Pico della Mirandola. In the sixteenth century Calcidius continued to be cited by students of Plato's *Timaeus*, though Ficino's *Compendium in Timaeum* (1496) replaced it as the standard commentary. The *editio princeps* appeared in Paris in 1520, edited by the Genoese Dominican Agostino Giustiniani (Hankins 2003-04).

2. *Hermeias*

Hermeias of Alexandria was a Neoplatonist who flourished in the second half of the fifth century and taught in Alexandria. Some thirty codices of his *Scholia on the Phaedrus* survive; copies were owned by Bessarion, Lorenzo de' Medici, Diego Hurtado de Mendoza and Lucas Holstenius. The work was well known to Ficino, who quotes it on a number of occasions and drafted a translation of it (Allen 1995), but it was not printed until the 1901 edition of Paul Couvreur (Ficino 2001-06, Hermeias of Alexandria 1901).

3. *Proclus*

Proclus (ca. 412-ca. 495 AD) was the head of the Academy in Athens and the most important pagan Neoplatonic author of late antiquity. A large number of his works survive. In addition to his independent works on philosophical and theological subjects (see NEOPLATONISTS), he wrote numerous commentaries and lectures on Plato, five of which survive.

a. *Lectures on the Cratylus* (fragment). This text does not seem to have been cited by Ficino and was not, as far as is presently known, studied during the Renaissance. The Greek text was first published by J. F. Boissonade in 1820 (Proclus 1908).

b. *Commentary on the First Alcibiades*. The Greek text circulated widely in manuscript and was studied by Francesco Patrizi da Cherso and Lucas Holstenius among others (Proclus 1985-86). Long excerpts were translated by Ficino around 1488 and published in 1497 by Aldus (Kristeller 1938). About half of the text was translated by Nicolaus Scutellius of Trent (Monfasani 2005), but the version remained in manuscript and was not published until 1820.[5] The Greek text too was not published until the nineteenth century.

c. The *Commentary on the Parmenides* was translated by William of Moerbeke in the late thirteenth century (Brams and Vanhamel 1989) and studied by philosophers from Aquinas to Nicholas of Cusa; in the sixteenth century it was annotated by Caesar Rovidius (d. 1594), a professor of medicine in Milan and there was another copy at the Collegio Romano in Rome. But the Moerbeke version was not published until the twentieth century (Proclus 1982-85). In 1521 a new version was made by Nicolaus Scutellius, a *protégé* of Giles of Viterbo, the General of the Augustinian Order (Monfasani 2005), but the version remained in manuscript until 1820. The Greek text was known to and used by Ficino.

d. The first twelve treatises of the *Commentary on the Republic* were known to and used by Ficino after 1492 (Allen 1994). This first part only of the Greek text was printed in Simon Grynaeus' 1534 edition of Plato from a manuscript in Corpus Christi College, Oxford, once owned by William Grocyn (Proclus 1899). The last five treatises were known in manuscript from the mid-sixteenth century (Lucas Holstenius was among those with access to the Vatican copy) but they were not printed until 1886 (Whittaker 1973). Extracts relating to Homer were translated by Conrad Gesner in a publication of 1542.

e. Extracts from the *Commentary on the Timaeus* were translated by William of Moerbeke before 1274 (Brams and Vanhamel 1989); another extract was translated into Latin and published by Niccolò Leonico Tomeo in 1525 in his *Opuscula nuper in lucem aedita* and republished in a 1530 edition of the Aris-

---

[5] To the information assembled by Monfasani it may be added that Scutellius' translations of Proclus' commentaries on the *Parmenides* and *Alcibiades* I were both printed by Victor Cousin in his 1820 and 1864 editions of Proclus' works; Cousin falsely ascribes the translations to Antonius Hermannus Gogava (BRAMS and VANHAMEL 1989, pp. 359-360; PROCLUS 1985-86, 1: CXXXVII-CXXXVIII).

totle's *Parva Naturalia*. The Greek text was known to Ficino, who cites it frequently in his *Platonic Theology* and *Compendium in Timaeum*; this commentary too was first published in Simon Grynaeus' 1534 edition of Plato's works from a manuscript in Corpus Christi College, Oxford, once owned by William Grocyn (Proclus 1903).

4. *Damascius*

Damascius (b. ca. 462) studied in Alexandria and for a while was the head of the Academy in Athens. In addition to his commentaries on Plato, an independent work, the *De principiis*, survives (see NEOPLATONISTS). His commentary on the *Parmenides* survives in a single manuscript left to the Biblioteca Marciana in Venice by Bessarion and was not published until 1889 (Damascius 1997). The anonymous *Lectures on the Philebus* and the anonymous monograph on the argument from opposites in the *Phaedo* (once attributed to Olympiodorus but attributed to Damascius in modern times by L. G. Westerink) circulated in manuscript, including copies owned by Bessarion, Ficino, Diego Hurtado de Mendoza, Sebastiano Erizzo, and Francesco Patrizi da Cherso but the Greek texts were not printed until the nineteenth century (Damascius 1959; Damascius and Olympiodorus 1976-77).

5. *Olympiodorus*

Olympiodorus (b. ca. 495/505-d. after 565) was a representative of Alexandrian Neoplatonism and the last pagan to teach in the Academy in that city. A number of works survive (see NEOPLATONISTS), including three commentaries on dialogues of Plato, the *First Alcibiades*, the *Gorgias* and the *Phaedo*. For the commentary on the *Philebus* once attributed to him see DAMASCIUS; for his commentary on Aristotle's *Meteora* see ARISTOTLE, COMMENTATORS. None of the Plato commentaries was edited or translated in the Renaissance but the Greek texts circulated in manuscript. Copies were annotated by Bessarion (who quotes them in his *In calumniatorem Platonis* of 1469) and by Ficino (who quotes them in his *Platonic Theology* of 1482); in the sixteenth century other copies belonged to Diego Hurtado de Mendoza, Sebastiano Erizzo, Francesco Patrizi da Cherso, and Lucas Holstenius. The *Commentary on the First Alcibiades* contains the *Vita Platonis*, sometimes printed as a separate work (see BIOGRAPHY). Further information on his Renaissance reception may be found in Schmitt 1971a.

V

ARISTOTLE, HIS SCHOOL AND HIS COMMENTATORS

A. ARISTOTLE

Aristotle (384-322 BC) is said to have written over one hundred and fifty books on logical, biological, physical, metaphysical and moral topics, of which about one-fifth survive. He enjoyed a unique popularity in the Middle Ages, becoming the backbone of university arts education, and saw virtually his entire surviving corpus and at least twenty-six spurious works translated into Latin by 1278 (Dod 1982; see PSEUDO-ARISTOTLE), together with a large body of commentary materials from Greek and Arabic sources. Medieval philosophers also composed a large number of new commentaries in Latin (Lohr 1967-74; Flüeler 1992; Thijssen and Braakhuis 1999; Lines 2002a). Medieval translations and commentaries on Aristotle continued to circulate widely in the Renaissance, especially in university settings.

In the fifteenth and sixteenth century, humanists undertook to retranslate Aristotle into a more classical form of Latin. The translations are too numerous to list individually, as the scale of Renaissance translation activity with respect to Aristotle's works dwarfs even that of the Middle Ages. Between the twelfth and fourteenth centuries about two dozen translators produced about 85 Latin translations of Aristotelian and pseudo-Aristotelian works which are preserved in about 2000 manuscripts (many of them copied in the fifteenth century); but between 1400 and 1600 about 70 translators produced more than 275 Latin translations of the same works which are preserved in several thousand manuscripts and hundreds of printed editions (Dod 1982; Cranz and Schmitt 1984). Even this accounting understates the influence of Renaissance scholarship on the presentation of Aristotle's philosophy in Latin, since many medieval translations were reprinted with extensive revisions and corrections made by Renaissance humanists. Humanist versions gradually displaced medieval ones, beginning with moral philosophy. In the manuscript period Leonardo Bruni's humanist translations of the *Ethics* (1416-17), *Eco-*

nomics (1420) and *Politics* (1436) were already more popular than the medieval versions, surviving in 285, 260 and 206 manuscripts respectively – a number greater than the total of all the extant manuscripts containing translations of Aristotle's moral works from the Middle Ages (Hankins 1997). In the incunabular period, one third of the print editions of the *Nicomachean Ethics*, *Politics* and *Economics* used the old translations and two thirds the new, while in the sixteenth century the old translations accounted for only a quarter of the editions of the *Economics* and less than one in twenty of the *Politics* and *Nicomachean Ethics*. Humanist translations of the *Rhetoric*, particularly that of George of Trebizond, also rapidly replaced Moerbeke's medieval version. Aristotle's *Poetics* was retranslated by Georgio Valla (1498) to replace Moerbeke's rendering, but in the sixteenth century the most popular version was that of Alessandro de' Pazzi, first printed in 1536 (Cranz and Schmitt 1984).

Humanist versions of the scientific and logical works took longer to displace the medieval versions, but the tipping point had been reached by the middle of the sixteenth century. For example, of the sixteenth-century editions of *De anima*, forty percent were in John Argyropoulos' humanist version, one quarter in medieval versions, fifteen percent in versions by minor translators, and twenty percent in the translation of Joachim Périon, first published in 1549, whose Ciceronian renderings of Aristotle's complete works became popular in the latter half of the sixteenth century. Similarly, nearly half the printings of the *Physics* and *De caelo* in the sixteenth century were in Argyropoulos' translations, one-quarter were in the medieval versions of Michael Scot and William of Moerbeke, and one quarter in the Périon version. *De generatione et corruptione* was published forty percent of the time in the humanist version of François Vatable, a royal lecturer in Paris, and twenty percent each in the Périon and the medieval translation. The *Meteorologica* was published roughly one quarter of the time in the Périon edition, one quarter in the Vatable translation, and twenty percent in the medieval version, while assorted other translations account for the remaining thirty percent. The *Metaphysics* was almost always printed in Bessarion's version, but sometimes in Moerbeke's translation accompanied by Averroes' commentary. Aristotle's logical works were treated with the greatest conservatism, and Boethius' translations continued to account for more than half of the Latin editions of the *Organon* and its constituent works throughout the sixteenth century, no doubt in part owing to Boethius' greater prestige as an ancient author (Cranz and Schmitt 1984).

The first Greek edition of Aristotle was the five-volume folio *Opera* printed by Aldus Manutius in 1495-98. This provides a good snapshot of the Aristotelian canon in the High Renaissance and shows the extent to which genuine works were mingled with *spuria* (see PSEUDO-ARISTOTLE). Volume I contained the complete *Organon* including PORPHYRY'S *Isagoge*. Volume II collected the *Physics, De caelo, De generatione et corruptione, Meteorologica* and the pseudo-Aristotelian *De mundo*. Volume III contained the five works on animals, the nine sections of the *Parva Naturalia*, plus *De anima* and six spurious works: the *De spiritu, De coloribus, Physionomia, De mirabilibus ascultationibus, De lineis insecabilibus*, and *De Xenophane, Zenone et Gorgia*. Volume IV contained the *Metaphysics* as well as the spurious *Mechanica* and *Problemata*, while the last volume contained the *Politics, Economics*, and the *Nicomachean Ethics* with its two companions, the *Eudemian Ethics* and *Magna Moralia*, the latter now doubtfully attributed to Aristotle. These volumes also contained a range of supplementary texts in Greek, including a life of Aristotle attributed to JOHN PHILOPONUS, DIOGENES LAERTIUS' lives of Aristotle and Theophrastus (see BIOGRAPHY), Galen's *De philosopho historia* (see DOXOGRAPHIES AND ANTHOLOGIES), Philo Judaeus' treatise *De mundo*, two books of spurious *Problemata* attributed to ALEXANDER APHRODISIENSIS and twelve treatises of THEOPHRASTUS, including the *Metaphysics*, which in the Middle Ages had sometimes been ascribed to Aristotle under the title *De principiis* (see THEOPHRASTUS). Aristotle's complete works were printed in Greek nine times in the sixteenth century (as compared with about 25 times in Latin), while most of the individual works were printed in Greek between seven and seventeen times, the exceptions being the *Nicomachean Ethics* (36 times) and *De anima* (21 times). The *Poetics*, the *Rhetoric* and the pseudonymous *Rhetorica ad Alexandrum* were first published in another Aldine collection, *Rhetores Graeci*, in 1508 and frequently republished (Cranz and Schmitt 1984).

In the vernacular, it was Aristotle's moral and literary works that were the most popular. The *Nicomachean Ethics* for example was available in Italian compendia from the later thirteenth century, in French from the later fourteenth century in a version by Nicole Oresme (first printed in 1488), in Spanish from 1489, in English from 1547. The *Politics* was available in three French translations: Oresme's (printed in 1489), Louis Le Roy's (1562) and Fédéric Morel's (1599). An English version was translated from Le Roy's French in 1597, an Italian version by Bernardo Segni appeared in 1549, and two Spanish versions, that of Carlos, Prince of Viana, and Pedro Simon Abril, appeared in 1509 and 1584 respectively. The complete *Rhetoric* was published in five separate Italian translations before 1600, and the *Poetics* saw three sixteenth-century Italian versions, those of Bernardo Segni (1549), Lodovico Castelvetro (1570), and Alessandro Piccolomini (1572). The scientific works appeared much more rarely in the vernacular, though there were two Italian translations of the *De anima*, Francesco Sansovino's in 1551 and Antonio Brucioli's in 1557. It is perhaps not surprising, given the technical and scholastic character of the work, that the *Organon* was not translated into any vernacular language during the Renaissance (Cranz and Schmitt 1984).

Medieval commentaries continued to be popular in the Renaissance: Aquinas' various commentaries were printed nineteen times in the incunabular period; Giles of Rome's sixteen times; Duns Scotus' eleven times; Albert the Great's ten times and Ockham's twice. Arabic commentaries reached the apogee of their influence in the sixteenth century (Hasse 2007), but there were already more than a dozen imprints containing Averroes' commentaries in Latin before 1500. However, the most important innovation of the Renaissance as regards the commentary tradition on Aristotle was the recovery of the ancient Greek commentators (see COMMENTATORS). Hundreds of new commentaries as well as other forms of Aristotelian literature were also composed by both humanists and scholastics (Schmitt 1983a; Lohr 1988; Perfetti 2000; Lines 2002a). The most important Aristotelian commentators among the scholastics included Crisostomo Javelli, Agostino Nifo, Paul of Venice, Benedict Pereira, Joachim Périon, Francesco Piccolomini, Jacopo Zabarella, Marcantonio Zimara and the authors of the Coimbra commentaries (Doyle 2007), while the leading humanist commentators were Donato Acciaiuoli, Jacques Lefèvre d'Etaples, Philipp Melanchthon, Pier Vettori, Marc-Antoine Muret and Antonio Riccobono (Lines 2007). The vast majority of Pietro Pomponazzi's numerous commentaries on Aristotle remained unpublished in the Renaissance.

B. PSEUDO-ARISTOTLE

Both in terms of the number of manuscripts and printed editions and in terms of his philosophic impact, Pseudo-Aristotle can be considered one of the most influential authorities of the late Middle Ages and Renaissance. Works falsely attributed to Aristotle treat grammar, history, biography, medicine, magic, and astronomy as well as more the conventional subjects today associated with Aristotle such as logic, natural science and moral philosophy. The subject is, like all matters connected with the Renaissance Aristotle, vast and full of difficulties, but excellent bibliographical guidance is given by Schmitt and Knox 1985 and Cranz and Schmitt 1984, and more general observations on the role of pseudo-Aristotelian texts in medieval and Renaissance philosophy may be found in Kraye, Ryan and Schmitt 1986. In addition to the approximately 100 works in Latin attributed to Aristotle in the period before 1500 but not apparently based on Greek originals, there are about twenty which were regularly handed down with the Aristotelian corpus in Greek; most of these twenty are ancient and Peripatetic in origin. The most widely circulated pseudo-Aristotelian texts, however, were Arabic in origin: the *Liber de causis* (actually a compilation based on Plotinus and Proclus), the *Secretum secretorum* (a work on statecraft in the form of a letter from Aristotle to Alexander the Great), and the *De mineralibus* (a work which commonly circulated with the genuine *Meteorology*). A paraphrase of the *De mundo* continued to pass under the name of Apuleius, though there were also two medieval Latin translations; the work's attribution to Aristotle began to be widely questioned in the Renaissance (Kraye 2002). A number of pseudonymous works originally in Greek were newly translated into Latin during the Renaissance, of which the most important were the *De virtutibus* (1504), the *Mechanica* (1517), a key text for Renaissance engineers, and the *Theology of Aristotle* (1519), a compilation based on Plotinus (Kraye 2002). The most widely circulated commentary on a pseudonymous text was Leonardo Bruni's commentary on the *Economics* (Soudek 1968, 1976); the work most frequently translated into the vernacular was the *Secretum secretorum*, which was rendered into French (ca. 1500), English (1528), German (1530) and Italian (1568).

C. Theophrastus

Theophrastus succeeded Aristotle as the head of the Lyceum in 322 BC, and continued Aristotle's philosophical and scientific projects. He left more than two hundred works. Less than one tenth of his corpus survives today, but many works circulated in antiquity. The most complete surviving works are the *Characteres*, *De historia plantarum*, *De causis plantarum*, *Metaphysics*, *De igne* and *De lapidibus*. Significant fragments are preserved in Cicero, Aulus Gellius and Plutarch, and discussions appear in many other ancient authors, pagan and Christian. Jerome in particular made extensive use of Theophrastus; in his *Adversus Jovinianum* he preserved in Latin translation the *De nuptiis* fragment, the only substantial fragment to survive under Theophrastus' name in medieval Europe. After the thirteenth century Bartholomaeus de Messana's Latin translations of the fragmentary *De signis* (*De astrologia navali*), the *Metaphysics* (also called the *De principiis*) and *De coloribus* also circulated in Europe, all mistakenly attributed to Aristotle. The remaining corpus was preserved in Byzantine manuscripts, including fragments in the compilations of Stobaeus (see Doxographies and Anthologies) and Photius' *Bibliotheca*. In the sixth century the Neoplatonist Priscianus Lydus wrote a *Metaphrasis in Theophrastum*, which preserved the surviving fragments of the *De sensu* and *De phantasia et intellectu* (Schmitt 1971b).

With the exceptions noted, the surviving corpus was only brought to Western Europe in the fifteenth century, starting with Giovanni Aurispa's trips to Constantinople in 1421/23, during which he retrieved the botanical works and nine major fragments. Antonio Corbinelli (d. 1425) possessed a manuscript of the *Characteres* 1-15, and references to Theophrastus manuscripts appear in the correspondence of Ambrogio Traversari and Francesco Filelfo in the 1420s and 30s. *Characteres* 1-15 was translated into Latin by Lapo da Castiglionchio around 1434-35. Between 1447 and 1455 Pope Nicholas V commissioned Theodore Gaza to make translations of the botanical works; Gregorio Tifernate translated the *De igne, De vertigine, Metaphysics* and *De piscibus* (1453/55), also for Nicholas V, and Cardinal Bessarion made a third version of the *Metaphysics* (1447-53), which became the version most commonly printed (twelve times in the sixteenth century). Priscianus Lydus' *Metaphrasis in Theophrastum* was translated into Latin by Ficino in 1488 and his Latin version was published by Aldus in 1497; the Greek text was first printed in 1541. Theophrastus did not begin to assert a wide influence until the sixteenth century, but his fifteenth century readers include important figures such as Marsilio Ficino, Giovanni Pico della Mirandola and Ermolao Barbaro (Schmitt 1971b).

The first works printed in Greek were included as part of the 1495-98 Aldine edition of ARISTOTLE. Volume I contained DIOGENES LAERTIUS' life of Theophrastus; volume II Theophrastus' *De igne, De ventis, De signis aquarum et ventorum* and *De lapidibus*; volume III *De piscibus, De vertigine oculorum, De laboribus, De odoribus* and *De sudoribus*; and volume IV *De historia plantarum, De causis plantarum* and *Metaphysica*. The preface and chapters 1-15 of the *Characteres* were first printed in Greek in 1527, chapters 16-23 in 1552, and chapters 24-28 in 1599. An *Opera* of Theophrastus, edited by Giovanni Battista Camozzi and published in Venice in 1552, contained the first edition of the *De sensibus*, an important fragment omitted from most early *Opera* and widely ignored until the nineteenth century. In 1557 Henri Estienne (Henricus II Stephanus) in his *Aristotelis et Theophrasti scripta quaedam* printed in Greek the fragments from Photius' *Bibliotheca*, including *De animi defectione, De nervorum resolutione, De animalibus quae colorem mutant, De animalibus quae repente apparent*, and *De animalibus quae dicuntur invidere*. The seventeenth century was the true peak of Theophrastus' influence, with a Greek *Opera* in 1605 and another in 1613 edited by Daniel Heinsius. This would remain the standard edition for two centuries (Schmitt 1971b).

After the appearance of the Aldine Aristotle, the pace of translation and publication of Theophrastus' works increased markedly. The thirteenth-century translation of *De signis* by Bartholomaeus de Messana was printed in 1501 and thrice more before 1528, always under the name of Aristotle, despite the fact that the Greek text had been attributed to Theophrastus in the Aldine edition of 1497. The Latin translation of *Characteres* 1-15 by Lapo was first printed in 1517, though it was misattributed to Angelo Poliziano from its 1583 reprint on. A bilingual school edition of chapters 1-23 was published by Leonardus Lycius in 1561, and a bilingual edition of 1-28 by Isaac Casaubon in 1599. Six different complete or partial translations of the *Characteres* were printed in the sixteenth century. Adrien Turnèbe's translation of *De igne* was printed in 1553, his bilingual, annotated *De odoribus* in 1556, and his *De lapidibus* and *De ventis* posthumously in 1578 and 1600 respectively. A Latin *De ventis* and *De signis* by Fredericus Bonaventura, with commentary, appeared in 1593. Bonaventura Grangerius published Latin versions of *De sudore* and *De vertigine* with commentary in 1576. Conrad Gesner included a partial translation of the *De piscibus* in his edition of the *Historia Animalium* of 1558 (Schmitt 1971b).

The 1605 bilingual *Opera*, printed again in 1613, contained eighteen works with commentary, including seven works printed for the first time: *De animi defectione*, *De nervorum resolutione*, *De animalibus quae colorem mutant*, *De animalibus quae repente apparent*, *De animalibus quae dicuntur invidere*, and *De melle*, all in anonymous translations, plus Daniele Furlano's translation of *De lassitudine*, his translations of the entire fragment *De piscibus* and eight other works, and Adrien Turnèbe's *De igne*. There are two Renaissance translations of the *De sensibus* that survive in manuscript, but a translation was not printed until Wimmer's edition of 1866. The Greek original of the *Liber de nuptiis* fragment does not survive, but the Latin excerpt appeared in Jerome's *Adversus Jovinianum*; it was not printed with the works of Theophrastus until the end of the eighteenth century (Schmitt 1971b).

The *Characteres* soon established itself as the most widely-read work of Theophrastus. A school edition with a brief philological commentary was published by Leonardus Lycius in 1561, but the major edition was that of Isaac Casaubon, who published a translation with extensive commentary in 1592 (1-23) and 1599 (1-28); the latter edition was reprinted more than thirty times before 1800, and was a major influence on English and French literature in the seventeenth century. Of the minor and fragmentary works, the most popular was the *Metaphysics*, commonly printed with Aristotle's *Metaphysics*. For further details on spurious works, commentaries and vernacular translations one may consult Schmitt 1971b.

D. COMMENTATORS

At least twenty-two ancient writers who lived between the first century BC and the early seventh century AD have been identified as the authors of commentaries on the writings of Aristotle. The commentaries that survive, together with a quantity of Byzantine Aristotelian commentaries, have been collected in the 23 volumes (with 2 supplements) of *Commentaria in Aristotelem Graeca* (*CAG*), published by the Berlin Academy between 1882 and 1996 (Sorabji 1990). The five commentators treated below were by far the best known in the Renaissance.

1. *Alexander Aphrodisiensis*

Alexander of Aphrodisias (fl. 198-209 AD), a public teacher of Aristotelian philosophy, was the most important ancient commentator on Aristotle's works; his writings, consisting of both commentaries and independent treatises, were quoted extensively by writers in later antiquity. Of his commentaries there survive those on *Metaphysics I-IV*, *Prior Analytics I*, *Topics I-IV*, *Meteorologica*, and the *De sensu et sensatu*. A continuation of the *Metaphysics* commentary is spurious in its present form and a commentary on the *Sophistical Elenchus* attributed to him during the Renaissance is probably by the Byzantine Michael of Ephesus. Six of his independent treatises survive in Greek (*On the Soul I and II*,[6] *On Fate*, *On Mixtures*, *Physical Questions*, *Ethical Problems*), and at least 17 additional ones are preserved only in Arabic (Goulet 1989-2005). Some medical works, including the *De febribus*, and a collection of *Problemata* were also falsely attributed to him in the Renaissance.

Of the seventeen independent treatises preserved only in Arabic, two, the *De augmento* and *De motu et tempore*, were translated by Gerard of Cremona in the twelfth century; neither translation was published in the Renaissance. Gerard may also be the translator of the *De sensu et sensato* commentary and the *De intellectu* section of *De anima II*, completed around the same time. William of Moerbeke translated the commentaries on *De sensu* and *Meteorologica* in the thirteenth century, but these versions too were not printed in the Renaissance (Brams and Vanhamel 1989). The *De fato* and fragments of the spurious *Sophistic Elenchus* commentary were also rendered into Latin by unknown medieval translators. The *De intellectu* in particular was used by

---

[6] Book I of *De anima* is genuine but Book II seems to be a compilation of 25 or 27 short tractates from Alexander's school (CRANZ 1960, 77-135).

Thomas Aquinas and other scholastics interested in the Aristotelian theory of the intellect (Cranz 1960).

After this, little attention was paid to Alexander in the west until the late fifteenth century, when there was a revival of interest in his writings. Almost all of Alexander's works presently known were printed in Greek between 1513 and 1536, mostly by the Aldine Press. The first Aldine version was the 1513 commentary on the *Topica*. The commentaries on the *Prior Analytics* and the pseudo-Alexandrine *Sophistic Elenchus* were published in 1520. The *De sensu* commentary was printed with SIMPLICIUS' *In De anima* in 1527, and the same year *De mixtione* and the *Meteorologica* commentary were published with JOHN PHILOPONUS' *In De generatione*, *De fato* and *De anima I* and *II* (including *De intellectu* which is part of Book II) were printed in 1534 with the Aldine edition of Themistius. Finally, the *Quaestiones Naturales et Morales* were printed with the works of Damascius and others in 1536. The works on psychology were by far the most popular and were printed in many editions (Cranz 1960).

The *Metaphysics* commentary, first printed in 1847, was the only work of Alexander surviving in Greek which was not edited in the Renaissance. It was however, available in the Latin translation of Juan Sepulveda, published in 1527 and frequently reprinted. Other works of Alexander were printed in Latin versions much earlier. Hieronymus Donatus published his translation of *De anima I* in 1495, and the work saw at least thirteen editions by 1559 (Kraye 2003). The *Topics* commentary was translated by Marcus Musurus to accompany the Aldine edition of the Greek text (1513). *De anima II*, translated by Angelus Caninius, was printed four times from 1546 to 1559. A medieval translation of the *De intellectu* section of *De anima II*, attributed to Gerard of Cremona, was published in 1501 and at least three more times by 1528. A new translation of the *De intellectu* by Girolamo Bagolino was printed in 1516. Bagolino's translation of *De fato* was printed in 1516; other versions were made by Gentien Hervet (1544) and Hugo Grotius (1648). Latin versions of the *Meteorologica* commentary were made by Alexander Piccolomini (1540) and Giovanni Battista Camozzi (1556). The *De mixtione* was available in Latin after 1540. In 1541 Guilelmus Dorotheus published his translation of the spurious *Sophistic Elenchus* commentary, revised by Johannes Nabascunensis in 1542, as well as the genuine *Topica* commentary, revised anonymously in 1547. Both works were published in various Latin versions in the second half of the sixteenth century. The first complete translation of the *Quaestiones naturales et morales* was printed in Latin in 1541 in a translation by Bagolino and his son. The commentary on the *Prior Analytics* was printed four times between 1542 and 1560 in the translation of Johannes Bernardus Felicianus. The commentary on *De sensu* was published in Lucillus Philalthaeus' translation in 1544, 1549 and 1573 (Cranz 1960).

The most popular Alexandrine work after the psychological treatises was the spurious collection of *Problemata*. This existed in two different Greek forms: the shorter contained Books I and II only and was published in a Greek Aldine edition in 1497; the latter two books, sometimes falsely attributed to Aristotle, were not published in Greek until 1857. Books I and II had been translated into Latin as early as Peter of Abano's version of 1302. A version containing most of Books I-IV translated by Theodore Gaza for Pope Nicholas V in 1453 was published in 1503-4 and saw at least twenty editions by 1608, many in editions of Aristotle's works. Georgio Valla's *Problemata* translation, containing Books I, II and IV with minor additions and omissions, was first published in 1488, and was frequently reprinted; Angelus Politianus' version of Book I saw at least twenty-five editions between 1498 and 1601 (Cranz 1960). The work had a readership beyond learned audiences, appealing to persons interested in folk-lore and popular science, and "lowbrow" versions were published in Latin, German, French and English well into the eighteenth century (Blair 1999).

2. *Themistius*

Themistius (ca. 317-ca. 388) was a Greek philosopher and rhetorician who taught in Constantinople and enjoyed the favor of the imperial family despite his paganism. He composed a series of explanatory paraphrases of Aristotle's *Posterior Analytics*, *Physics*, *De anima* (which survive in Greek) and of the *De caelo* and *Metaphysics XII* (which survive in a medieval Hebrew version made from a lost Arabic translation). The medieval Latin world had only Gerard of Cremona's version of the *Posterior Analytics* paraphrase (late twelfth century) and William of Moerbeke's Latin rendering (1267) of the *De anima* summary (Brams and Vanhamel 1989). His works, many of which are now lost, were also known indirectly thanks to their use by Boethius, Cassiodorus and the medieval Arabic commentators on Aristotle, particularly Averroes. The *De anima* paraphrase was well known to scholastic philosophers and theologians (Todd 2003).

The Renaissance revival of Themistius was largely the work of Ermolao Barbaro, who between 1473 and 1480 produced fresh versions of the paraphrases on the *Posterior Analytics* and *De anima* as well as the first Latin version of the *Physics* paraphrase. These were first published in 1481 and frequently reprinted. He also translated as part of the corpus four spurious works, the paraphrases on the *De insomniis*, *De divinatione per somnum*, *De memoria et reminiscentia* and *De somno et vigilia*, all of which he believed to be genuine. The Hebrew version of the *Metaphysics XII* paraphrase was translated into Latin by Mosè Finzi after 1550 and was published in 1558 and 1576. A Latin translation of the *De caelo* paraphrase made from the medieval Hebrew version was first begun around 1561 by Mosè Alatino, a student of Francesco Piccolomini, and was published in 1574 (Todd 2003).

Greek manuscripts of Themistius circulated widely in the fifteenth century but the first Greek edition of his works was published in an Aldine *Opera* of 1534. The *De anima* paraphrase generated a number of commentaries, including those of the philosophers Marcantonio Zimara (1542), Lodovico Nogarola (1554), and Federico Pendasio (unpublished). Zimara also published a commentary on the *Physics* paraphrase in 1542. No translations of Themistius' works into a vernacular language were published during the Renaissance (Todd 2003).

3. *Ammonius*

Ammonius of Alexandria (ca. 440-ca. 517) was a student of Proclus in Athens who later taught in Alexandria, numbering John Philoponus among his students. He edited under his own name a course on Aristotle's *De interpretatione*, while notes from other courses given on PORPHYRY's *Isagoge*, on the *Categories* and on the *Prior Analytics* were collected by students (see PHILOPONUS). Other courses and independent treatises that do not survive are attested in ancient sources (Goulet 1989-2005, 168-170).

Nicholas Vlastos published the Greek text of the course on the *Isagoge* in 1500 and Aldus printed the course on the *De interpretatione* in 1503; Aldus also published under the name of Ammonius JOHN PHILOPONUS' course on the *Categories* (1503). The *Isagoge* course was translated into Latin by Pomponius Gauricius in 1526 and the *De interpretatione* was rendered into Latin by William of Moerbeke (1268) and Bartolomaeus Sylvanius in 1543 (Brams and Vanhamel 1989; Lohr 2000).

4. *Simplicius*

Simplicius, a pagan Neoplatonist who flourished in the sixth century AD, wrote important commentaries on Aristotle's *De caelo*, *Physics* and *Categories*. A fourth commentary on the *De anima* was universally ascribed to Simplicius until questioned by Francesco Piccolomini in 1602, and the attribution remains in doubt today (Hadot, I. 1987; Mahoney 1982). Simplicius also composed a commentary on EPICTETUS' *Manual* as well as some other works surviving in fragmentary form.

The first Simplician commentary to be printed in Greek was Nicholas Vlastos' 1499 edition of the *Categories* commentary. Aldine editions of the *Physics* and

De caelo commentaries followed in 1526; the latter text was actually a retranslation back into Greek of Moerbeke's Latin version, possibly made in Bessarion's circle, rather than the original Greek version; the latter was not published until the nineteenth century (Bossier 1987). The first Greek text of the *De anima* commentary to be printed was published by the heirs of Aldus in 1527, though the impact of that work began to be felt much earlier (Nardi 1958).

After Robert Grosseteste's translation of part of *De caelo II* (Bossier 1987), William of Moerbeke translated Simplicius' commentaries on the *Categories* (1266) and the *De caelo* (1271) into Latin (Brams and Vanhamel 1989). These translations had some influence in the later Middle Ages via Aquinas and other thinkers (Bossier 1987). Moerbeke's translation of the *Categories* commentary was printed in revised form in 1516. A fresh translation of this commentary was made in 1540 by Gulielmus Dorotheus. In the same year Moerbeke's translation of the *De caelo* commentary was published in revised form. Further revisions were made in the second edition of 1544, probably by the same Dorotheus; these are extensive enough to consider this redaction a new translation (Bossier 1987). Another translation was made by Evangelista Lungus and published in 1554. The *De anima* commentary was published in Johannes Faseolus' Latin version in 1543 and in Evangelista Lungus' Latin in 1553. The *Physics* commentary, confusingly referred to as a commentary "on the eight books *On the Physics of Hearing*" (*Commentaria in octo libros Aristotelis Stagiritae De physico auditu*), appeared in Latin versions by Lucillus Philaltheus (Lucilio Maggi) in 1543 and by Gentian Hervet in 1551.

5. *John Philoponus*

John Philoponus (ca. 490-570s AD), also called John the Grammarian, was a Christian Neoplatonist and theologian who taught in Alexandria. He was known in the Renaissance for his critique of Aristotelian physics, important for the development of early modern science, and for his philosophical defense of creation *ex nihilo* as well as his attempts to reconcile Plato and Aristotle (Schmitt 1989). He composed commentaries on Aristotle's *Categories*, *Prior Analytics*, *Posterior Analytics*, *Meteorology*, *On Generation and Corruption*, *On the Soul*, and *Physics*. Four of the commentaries are derived, as Philoponus tells us, from seminars with his teacher AMMONIUS, but with material added by Philoponus himself. Philoponus was also the author of various theological treatises on the Trinity and creation as well as two treatises *On the Eternity of the World* (see NEOPLATONISTS, PHILOPONUS); for the life of Aristotle attributed to him, see BIOGRAPHY.

Philoponus was well known in the Arabic world and some testimonia regarding him therefore made their way to the scholastic philosophers of the medieval Latin West. But the only work of his directly known to the medievals was the commentary on the *De anima*, of which a small portion, called *De intellectu* (=*De anima* 3.4-8) was translated by William of Moerbeke in 1268 (Brams and Vanhamel 1989). Though manuscripts of Philoponus circulated in the fifteenth century, knowledge of his works remained limited before the first half of the sixteenth century, during which virtually all of the extant commentaries of Philoponus became available in Greek editions and Latin translations (Schmitt 1989). The first work to be published in Greek was the *Categories* commentary, which appeared under the name of AMMONIUS in Aldus' edition of 1503. Greek editions followed of the commentaries on the *Posterior Analytics* (1504), *On Generation and Corruption* (1527), *Prior Analytics* (1535), *De anima* (1535), *Physics* (1535), and *Meteorology* (1551).

Latin translations of Philoponus' works, unusually, followed the publication of the Greek texts. From 1539 to 1544 the Venetian printers Octavianus and Hieronymus Scotus published Latin translations of most of the corpus of Philoponus, including the commentaries on the *Prior Analytics* and *Physics* by Gulielmus Dorotheus (1539), the *Posterior Analytics* by Andreas Gratiolus (1539, revised by Philippus Theodosius in 1542), *On Generation and Corruption* by Girolamo Bagolino (1540), *Categories* by Bartolomaeus Sylvanius (1541, attributed to Ammonius), and *De anima* by Matthaeus à Bove (1544). Gentian Hervet also published a translation of the *De anima* commentary at Lyon in the same year, 1544. A Latin translation of the commentary on the *Meteorology* I, by Giovanni Battista Camozzi, appeared with the *princeps* of the Greek in 1551. While the Greek texts were usually published only once, the Latin translations were published in anywhere from seven to twelve editions, attesting to the interest they aroused (Schmitt 1989; Lohr 2000).

A commentary on the *De generatione animalium*, ascribed to Philoponus in the Renaissance, is now ascribed to Michael of Ephesus; it was published in Greek under Philoponus' name in 1526 with a Latin translation by Theodore Gaza (d. 1478). An anonymous commentary on the *Metaphysics* was published in Latin translation by Francesco Patrizi in 1583 as a work of Philoponus. The Greek original of this work, now considered the work of unknown Byzantine author, perished in the fire at the Escorial library in 1651 (Lohr 2000; Philoponus [Pseudo] 1991).

6. *Olympiodorus*

See above under PLATO, COMMENTATORS. The only work of Olympiodorus printed in Greek or translated was his commentary on Aristotle's *Meteora*. Though known in the medieval Arabic and Byzantine worlds, the first known citation of it in the Latin West was by Gianfrancesco Pico della Mirandola in 1520. The Greek text was printed in Venice in 1551 to accompany a separate printing of the Latin translation by Giovanni Battista Camozzi; there is also an anonymous translation preserved in a single manuscript of the late sixteenth or early seventeenth century. The commentary was well known to students of meteorology in the later Renaissance (Schmitt 1971b).

VI

EPICUREANS

A. Epicurus

Epicurus (341-270 BC) is credited with at least forty-one works, none of which survives intact. The most important Greek source for his thought is Book X of Diogenes Laertius, which includes a biography of Epicurus, summaries of his ideas, a list of his works, his will, and three philosophical letters. Other fragments appear in various sources, including Plutarch, Porphyry, Lactantius, Simplicius, Alexander Aphrodisiensis, Sextus Empiricus, Athenaeus, Philodemus, Didymus Caecus, Clement of Alexandria, Aëtius, Stobaeus (see Doxographies and Anthologies), Origen, and Seneca's letters. Presentations of Epicurean philosophy of great importance for the Renaissance are found in the philosophical dialogues of Cicero, especially the *De natura deorum*, *Tusculan Disputations* and *Academica*. Our most important Latin source is the Roman Epicurean Lucretius, whose didactic poem *De rerum natura* presents Epicurus' philosophy in a way largely consistent with the doctrines outlined in Diogenes Laertius.

Epicurus' works were almost completely unknown in the medieval Latin West and indirect knowledge of his doctrines was often superficial and inaccurate (Pagnoni 1974; Murray 1986; Boter, forthcoming). Thanks partly to the recovery of Diogenes Laertius, however, the early Quattrocento made rapid strides in recovering Epicurus' thought (Garin 1979; Davies 1987; Lorch 1991; Fubini 2002). Suspicion of his philosophy remained constant, and even in 1601, when Nicholas Hill gave one of the first systematic presentations of Epicurean (and Democritean) philosophy, he was obliged to state that he was only "setting out" his doctrine, not teaching it.[7] For Gassendi's study of Epicurus, see Diogenes Laertius, below.

---

[7] Nicolaus Hill, *Philosophia Epicurea, Democritiana, Theophrastica, proposita simpliciter, non edocta*, Paris 1601 (Risse 1998, 7:67).

B. LUCRETIUS

Lucretius' (94-55/51 BC) long didactic poem on the Epicurean system is our largest and most complete classical source of Epicurean philosophy, and covers cosmological, theological and moral themes. Though several ninth century manuscripts survive, the *De rerum natura* had virtually no circulation in the later middle ages. Early in the fourteenth century there are signs that Lovato Lovati and Albertino Mussato may have read Lucretius (Billanovich 1958; but see Reeve 1980). The Renaissance made contact with Lucretius in 1417 when Poggio Bracciolini and his friend Bartolomeo da Montepulciano found a copy during their book-hunting expeditions to monastery libraries during the Council of Constance. Poggio sent his copy to the Florentine humanist Niccolò Niccoli, from whose copy descends many though by no means all of the 52 other fifteenth-century manuscripts (Reeve 1980). A number of manuscripts and incunables contain notes by well-known humanists such as Pomponio Leto (1458), Joannes Sulpitius Verulanus (1466), Bartolomeo Fazio (1470s), Giovanni Gioviano Pontano, Angelo Poliziano, Michele Marullo, Marcello Adriani, Bernardino Ceppellari (1506), and Machiavelli (Gordon 1962; Bertelli 1965; Reeve 1980). The philosopher Marsilio Ficino before 1457 wrote *commentariola* on Lucretius, which he later burnt; but what are probably fragments from the lost commentary survive in some of his early writings, especially the *De voluptate* and *De quattuor sectis philosophorum* (Kristeller 1938). The poet was also known indirectly through quotations and testimonia in the Church Fathers (Hadzsits 1935; Fleishmann 1971; La Brasca 1999). For Renaissance biographies of Lucretius see Solaro 2000.

In the incunabular period there were three editions, printed in Brescia (1473), Verona (1486), and Venice (1495). The work was printed many times in the sixteenth century, often in school editions, the most popular texts being those established by Andrea Navagero (1515) and Denys Lambin (1562-63). The lone Renaissance translation of Lucretius into a vernacular language was Gianfrancesco Muscettola's translation into Italian verse made in 1530; this remained in manuscript. The first English translation did not appear until 1683 (Fleischmann 1971; Gordon 1962).

There were three printed Renaissance commentaries on Lucretius. The first was by Johannes Baptista Pius, published in 1511 and 1514. The second was the 1562-63 commentary of Denys Lambin, who also lectured on Lucretius in Paris, and whose edition, containing over 100,000 words of commentary, would remain the definitive Lucretius until the time of Lachmann. The third commentary was that of Obertus Gifanius, published in 1565 (Fleischmann 1971). A paraphrase of Book I was composed by Raffaele Franceschi in 1504

(Pizzani 1986), and a first attempt to extract Epicurean doctrine from Lucretius was made by Girolamo Frachetta in 1589.[8] The *De rerum natura* was imitated widely by Renaissance poets, from Pontano, Poliziano and Marullo to the poets of the Pléiade and Torquato Tasso (Prosperi 2004).

---

[8] *Breve spositione di tutta l'opera di Lucretio, nella quale si disamina la dottrina di Epicuro*, Venice 1589 (Risse 1998, 7:58).

VII

STOICS

The Stoic school was founded by Zeno of Citium (335-263 BC), and continued by Cleanthes (331-270 BC) and Chrysippus (280-207 BC) as well as by later figures, of whom the best known (thanks to Cicero) were Posidonius and Panaetius. The works of the early Stoics survive almost entirely in fragmentary form (Von Arnim 1903-24; Panaetius 1952; Posidonius 1989), so the main point of entry into early Stoicism for the Renaissance was indirect, through the works of CICERO, DIO CHRYSOSTOM, DIOGENES LAERTIUS, Galen (see DOXOGRAPHIES), PLUTARCH, the Greek COMMENTATORS on ARISTOTLE, SEXTUS EMPIRICUS, Joannes Stobaeus (see DOXOGRAPHIES) and the Church Fathers. Most familiar to Renaissance readers was the moral philosophy of the Stoics of the late Roman republic and early empire, especially SENECA, EPICTETUS and MARCUS AURELIUS. The first account of Stoicism as a philosophical system was provided by Justus Lipsius in his *Manuductio ad Stoicam philosophiam* and *Physiologia Stoicorum* of 1604, which was followed in 1606 by Kaspar Schoppe's *Elementa philosophiae stoicae moralis*. Of less interest philosophically was Guillaume Du Vair's *La philosophie morale des stoïques* (1585), of which an English version was made by Thomas James and published in 1598. A Stoic logic was reconstructed from the works of Cicero by Adamus Bursius in 1604.[9]

A. SENECA

Before the seventeenth century Lucius Annaeus Seneca the Younger (4 BC-65 AD), the moral philosopher and tragedian, was not firmly distinguished

---

[9] *Dialectica Ciceronis, quae disperse in scriptis reliquit, maxime ex Stoicorum sententia, cum commentariis quibus ea partim supplentur, partim illustrantur*, Zamosz 1604 (RISSE 1998, 2:228).

from his father, Lucius Annaeus Seneca the rhetorician. But from the time of Petrarch forward it was debated whether Seneca the moral philosopher should be distinguished from Seneca the tragedian (Fohlen 2002). The spurious letters of Seneca to St. Paul, whose authenticity was affirmed by Jerome, made him a kind of pagan saint in the eyes of the Latin West. In addition to the tragedies and the *Apocolocyntosis*, a satire on the emperor Claudius, there survive five large philosophical works, all widely circulated in the Middle Ages. These include the *Dialogi* (ten treatises on ethics including *On Anger* in three books, *On Providence*, *On the Constancy of the Wise Man*, *To Marcia on Consolation*, *To Polybius on Consolation*, *To Helvia on Consolation*, *On the Blessed Life*, *On Tranquillity of Soul*, *On Leisure*, and *On the Shortness of Life*), *On Clemency*, *On Favors* in seven books, *Natural Questions*, and the *Moral Letters* (124 letters in 20 books). A number of other philosophical works have been lost but were quoted or referred to in antiquity, particularly by Lactantius, Jerome and Augustine. The *Dialogues*, *On Clemency*, *On Favors*, and *Moral Letters* were continuously in print from 1475 onwards; the *Natural Questions* were first printed in 1490.

Seneca also enjoyed popularity in the vernacular, especially in his native Spain, and a Spanish version including his moral works was printed as early as 1491 (translated by Alonso of Cartagena, frequently reprinted). An Italian translation of the *Moral Letters*, made by Sebastiano Manilio, was printed in 1494; Benedetto Varchi translated the *On Favors* in 1554; and 1569 saw publication of Francesco Serdonati's Italian translation of the *De ira*. In 1536 Michael Herr published German translations of most of the moral works (Worstbruck 1976). Laurent de Premierfait's early fifteenth-century translation of "les Euvres de Seneque" was printed around 1500. A French translation of *On Favors* appeared in 1561, of the *Moral Letters* in 1582 and the complete philosophical works were published in 1590 in the translation of Simon Goulart. Nicholas Haward published an English version of *On Favors* in 1569, and Arthur Goldying made an English translation of the same text, printed in 1578.

As in the case of Plato, Aristotle and other authors, spurious works were an important part of Seneca's reception in the Renaissance. The six most important *spuria* are the *De paupertate*, *De remediis fortuitorum*, *De quattuor virtutibus cardinalibus*, *De moribus*, *Proverbia*, and *Epistulae Pauli et Senecae*.[10] All these short works circulated widely in manuscript and in three or four

---

[10] For the *De copia verborum* and *De legalibus instrumentis* and other pseudoepigrapha known in the manuscript era see FOHLEN 2002, 16-17.

times the number of printed editions as contain Seneca's genuine works; some or all were translated into Italian, French, German and Spanish, usually in advance of the genuine works. Erasmus' editions of Seneca (1515, 1529) were the first to identify *De quattuor virtutibus*, *Proverbia*, *De moribus* and *Epistolae Pauli et Senecae* as spurious, though he continued to list the *De paupertate* and *De remediis* among Seneca's genuine works and failed to distinguish between the elder and the younger Seneca (Reynolds 1965).

Renaissance commentaries on Seneca remain to be studied in detail. For commentaries in manuscript on the *Moral Letters* see Fohlen 2002; the most important was that of Gasparino Barzizza (Panizza 1977). The most important commentaries in print appear to be Matthaeus Fortunatus' notes on the *Natural Questions* (1522), John Calvin's commentary on the *On Clemency* (1532), the annotations of Marc-Antoine Muret on Seneca's prose works (1585), Muret's and Janus Gruterus' notes of 1592; and those contained in the edition of Justus Lipsius (1605).

B. DIO CHRYSOSTOM

Dio Chrysostom or Dio Cocceianus (ca. 40/50 AD-after 110) was a popular philosopher and rhetorician influenced primarily by Stoicism and Cynicism. His surviving works consist of eighty discourses (two of which, 37 and 64, are actually by his disciple Favorinus) on a wide variety of literary and philosophical topics. These began to be translated into Latin in the fifteenth century. Discourse 11 was translated by Filelfo (under the title *Oratio ad Ilienses*) in 1428 and was printed in 1492. Of more interest philosophically were the first four discourses, all entitled *On Kingdom* (*De regno*), which were translated by Gregorio Tifernate (1447/55) and by Andreas Brentius (1471/84), though the latter did not circulate widely. Giorgio Merula (d. 1494) translated discourses 70-72 (*On Philosophy*, *On the Philosopher*, *On the Philosopher's Dress*). A Latin translation of the *De regno* discourses by Francesco Todeschini Piccolomini, the future Pope Pius III, was printed in 1471 and 1493; Discourse 74, *On Distrust*, was translated by Joachim Camerarius in 1531; Discourses 6 and 66, *Against Tyranny* and *On Glory*, translated by Bartolomaeus Amantius, were printed in 1545. The *editio princeps* of all eighty discourses appeared in Venice in 1551; the first complete Latin translation was made by Thomas Naogeorgus (or Kirchmeier) and was published in 1555. Discourse 52, *Against Monarchy*, translated by Caelius Secundus Curio, appeared in a Latin edition of Machiavelli's *Prince* in 1580 as an "antidote" to the Florentine's theories.

A French edition of Discourse 62 (*Discours de la royauté et de la tyrannie*), translated by Fédéric Morel, was published in Paris in 1589; Discourse 65, under the title *Loüange de la loy*, was published in a translation by Dion Bouchedor in 1598.

C. EPICTETUS

Epictetus (mid-first to second century AD) taught Stoic philosophy in Rome until the time of Domitian, then relocated his school to Nicopolis in the Epirus. His works, written in Greek, include the *Discourses*, supposedly verbatim reports of his teaching collected by his student Arrian, and the brief *Enchiridion* or *Handbook*, which was also probably compiled by Arrian though it passes under Epictetus' own name. A commentary on the *Enchiridion* was composed by SIMPLICIUS, which proved far more popular in the Renaissance and seventeenth century than his better-known commentaries on Aristotle. A number of fragments of the lost *Diatribes* are preserved in Stobaeus (see DOXOGRAPHIES AND ANTHOLOGIES). Epictetus' views are also dubiously reported in a question-and-answer dialogue written in Latin in the second or third century AD, the *Altercation of the Emperor Hadrian and Epictetus*. This was first published in 1510 with the forgeries of Annius of Viterbo. Two other shorter works of similar content also circulated in manuscript.

In 1450 Niccolò Perotti, a humanist of Bessarion's circle, produced a Latin translation of the *Enchiridion* and the preface to Simplicius' commentary, dedicated to Pope Nicholas V; this survives in nineteen manuscripts but was not printed until modern times (Oliver 1954; Boter, forthcoming). It was Angelo Poliziano's translation, completed in 1479 and dedicated to Lorenzo the Magnificent, that first made the work widely known to Renaissance readers. It was first printed in 1497 in a miscellany compiled by Filippo Beroaldo and was reprinted 40 times before 1750. Eventually it was rivalled though not replaced by the Latin versions of Hieronymus Verlenius (1543), Thomas Naogeorgus or Kirchmeier (1554) and Hieronymus Wolf (1561). Wolf's translation eventually established itself as standard and was reprinted 68 times before 1750. The *Discourses* were translated twice in six years, by Jacob Schenck (1554) and Hieronymus Wolf (1563); both versions remained popular. Wolf's edition also included the first Latin translation of Simplicius' commentary on the *Enchiridion* (Boter, forthcoming).

The *editio princeps* of the *Enchiridion* in Greek was included with the 1528 Venice edition of Simplicius' commentary on the text. The *Discourses* had their *editio princeps* in 1535.

The earliest vernacular translation is the German translation of the *Enchiridion* by Jacob Schenck, published in 1534 (facsimile edition in Oldfather 1927). Antoine Du Moulin published the first French version of the *Enchiridion* in 1544, and the *Discourses* were gallicized by Jean Goulu in 1609. An Italian version of the *Enchiridion*, translated by Giulio Ballino, was published in 1564. James Sanford translated the *Enchiridion* into English in 1567. A Dutch translation of the same text was published by M. A. Gillis in 1564 (Boter, forthcoming). Francisco Anton de Sousa made a Portuguese translation, printed in 1594, and Francisco Sánchez de las Brozas (the rhetoric teacher from Salamanca, not the skeptical philosopher) published a Spanish translation of the same text in 1600.

The best known commentary on the *Enchiridion* was that of Simplicius, published at least nine times between 1528 and 1600. Thomas Naogeorgus (Kirchmaier) composed a commentary on the *Enchiridion* in 1554 dealing with ethical and religious issues, but the most important Renaissance study of the text was that of Hieronymus Wolf, printed with his bilingual (Greek and Latin) edition of Epictetus, Arrian's *Discourses* and Simplicius' commentary. Christian Francken's 1585 translation of the *Enchiridion* is also accompanied by a voluminous commentary based on that of Naogeorgus (Boter, forthcoming).

D. Marcus Aurelius

The *Meditations* of the emperor Marcus Aurelius (121-180 AD) were the least well known of the major sources for Stoic ethics during the Renaissance. There were only two complete Greek codices of the work. It was first mentioned in the Latin West by Johannes Reuchlin in his *De arte cabbalistica* of 1517, and was not published until 1559. In that year Gulielmus Xylander (Wilhelm Holtzmann) published a Greek text with Latin translation; it was republished with corrections in 1568. The work seems to have had little impact on Lipsius' presentation of Stoic philosophy (see STOICS), possibly because Xylander failed to identify the work as an example of Stoic philosophy. The work was first exploited as a source for Stoic philosophy by Isaac Casaubon in the early seventeenth century, in his 1605 commentary on Persius. The only sixteenth century translation was the French version of Pardoux Duprat, published in 1570. The first English version (1634) was that of Meric Casaubon,

4

son of Isaac, who gave the work its modern title *Meditations*. There were no commentaries made during the Renaissance apart from Xylander's (mostly philological) notes. *The Golden Book of Marcus Aurelius*, a "crude forgery" by Antonio de Guevara, was first published in Spanish in 1528 and frequently reprinted and translated into other vernaculars (Kraye 2002).

VIII

SKEPTICS

A. ACADEMIC SKEPTICISM AND CICERO

Several generations after Plato's death the Academy took a skeptical turn under the leadership of Arcesilaus (316-242 BC) and Carneades (214-129 BC). See OLD ACADEMY AND MIDDLE PLATONISM. The Academy continued to espouse a moderate skepticism down to the time of Philon of Larissa (159/158-83/84 BC), the teacher of Cicero and the last undisputed head of the Academy. The early academic skeptics are known only in fragments, primarily through the writings of Cicero. Another important source for Academic Skepticism for Renaissance readers was Augustine's *Contra Academicos*, based mostly on Cicero, which put about the perverse view that the school actually consisted of dogmatic Platonic realists concealing their true views under a skeptical disguise.

Cicero described himself as an Academic Skeptic, though he had a profound respect for ARISTOTLE and PLATO and was well-informed about Hellenistic philosophy, for which he is a major source. During his period of study in Greece he heard lectures from the Epicurean philosophers Phaedrus and Zeno, the Academic Skeptics Philon of Larissa and Antiochus of Ascalon, and the Stoic Posidonius. His dialogues often pit interlocutors belonging to different schools against each other, thus illustrating their various positions and arguments. His philosophical works include writings on political philosophy as well as works on epistemology, ethics and theology. *On the Commonwealth* (*De republica*) survives only in fragments, most of them recovered from a palimpsest in the early nineteenth century; the only substantial portion known to Renaissance readers was the *Dream of Scipio*, part of the sixth book, which was preserved in MACROBIUS' Platonizing commentary. *On Laws* preserves Stoic teaching on natural law. Stoic moral teaching is preserved in the *Paradoxes of the Stoics*, and Academic epistemological doctrine on the criterion of truth, particularly that of Arcesilaus and Carneades, is presented in the *Academica*. On the skeptical ground of preferring the views with the greatest verisimilitude, Cicero preferred the teaching of the STOICS to the EPICUREANS in *On the Ultimate Ends of Goods and Evils*, a dialogue on the highest good, and in the *Tusculan Disputations*, a dialogue about the psychology of the happy life. Cicero also prefers Stoic theological views in his dialogue between a Stoic, an Epicurean and an Academic *On the Nature of the Gods*, while in his *De divinatione* and the fragmentary *De fato* he decides against the Stoics, nevertheless giving a full account of their positions. Included in the class of moral works are his popular essays *On Old Age* and *On Friendship*. A treatise entitled *Topics* summarizes ARISTOTLE'S work on the same subject, and Cicero also undertook a translation of PLATO'S *Timaeus*, of which the first third survives. BOETHIUS composed a commentary on Cicero's *Topics* which was first printed in 1484 and frequently reprinted. Cicero's most famous and popular work, *On Duties*, is based on Stoic moral teaching, particularly that of Panaetius.

All of these works were preserved in many manuscripts of the High Middle Ages and early Renaissance and there are numerous glossed copies and commentaries which have not yet been fully explored by modern research. Cicero's were among the first works to be printed and remained easily available thereafter throughout the Renaissance in innumerable printings. The *On Duties* and *Paradoxes of the Stoics* were first published in 1465, *On Old Age* and *On Friendship* in 1467, the *Tusculan Disputations* in 1469, and in 1470 *Scipio's Dream* and *On Duties*. The first collection of Cicero's *philosophica*, including the *On the Nature of the Gods*, *On Divination*, *On Fate*, *Academica*, and *On Laws* was published in 1471; the *Topics* followed in 1472. The first *Opera omnia* was published in 1498-99.

The scale of Cicero's popularity in the Renaissance is indicated by the number of incunabula: *On Duties* was published in no fewer than 64 editions before 1500; *On Old Age* (65 editions), *On Friendship* (65), the *Paradoxes of the Stoics* (69) were even more popular. The *Somnium Scipionis* saw 28 printings with works of Cicero and six with Macrobius. Less popular were the *Tusculan Disputations* (16 editions), the *Timaeus* (11), the *Topics* (10), *On Fate* (9), *On Laws*, *On Ultimate Ends*, *On the Nature of the Gods* (8 each), *On Divination* and *Academica* (6 each) (Flodr 1973).

The first published translations were into English. John Tiptoft translated *On Friendship* into English in 1481, in an edition that also included *On Old Age*, translated (probably) by William Caxton from a French manuscript version by Laurent de Premierfait. Robert Whittington's *On Duties* and *Paradoxes* both appeared in 1534, followed by his *On Old Age* in 1535. Nicolas Grimald englished *On Duties* in 1556, a version frequently reprinted, and John Dolman the *Tusculan Disputations* in 1561. John Harington of Stepney translated the *On Friendship* into English from the French in 1550. Thomas Newton published English versions of *On Old Age* and the *Paradoxes* in 1569, *On Friendship* and the *Dream of Scipio* in 1577.

An anonymous German translation of *On Duties* was printed in the incunabular period (1488). The first German translations of the sixteenth century were of *On Old Age*, *On Friendship*, *Tusculan Disputations* (1522); this "Teütsch Cicero" was followed by German versions of *On Duties* (1531), the *Dream of Scipio* (1538), and the *Paradoxes* (1538) (Worstbruck 1976). A Dutch translation of *On Duties* by Dierick Coornhert was published in 1561.

Italian translations of Cicero's *philosophica* circulated in manuscript from the fourteenth century onwards, but published versions only began to appear in the 1520s. An Italian translation by Federico Vendramino of *On Duties*, *On Friendship*, *On Old Age* and the *Paradoxes* was published in 1528; the *Dream of Scipio* translated by Antonio Brucioli appeared in 1539; another version by Pompeo della Barba appeared in 1553; and Sebastiano Fausto da Longiano's version of the *Tusculan Disputations* came out in 1544. An Italian *Topics* was made by Simone della Barba in 1556. Ludovico Dolce published a corrected version of Vendramino's *volgare* translation of the *On Duties*, *On Friendship*, *On Old Age*, and *Paradoxes* in 1564.

Laurent de Premierfait made French translations of *On Old Age* (1405) and *On Friendship* (1416) which circulated in manuscript but were never printed during the Renaissance. An anonymous French translation of *On Duties* appeared in 1493/94, reprinted in 1538, followed by a 1539 edition of *On Duties*, *On Friendship*, *On Old Age*, the *Paradoxes*, and the *Dream of Scipio*, all translated by Denis Janot. Etienne Dolet translated the *Tusculan Disputations*, printed in 1543 and 1545; a new French translation of *On Friendship* by Blaise de Vigenère appeared in 1579.

A 1546 imprint contains Castilian versions by Francisco Tamara of Cadiz of *On Duties*, *On Friendship*, and *On Old Age* and this collection was frequently reprinted; in 1549 the collection was enlarged with versions of the *Paradoxes* and the *Dream of Scipio* by Juan Jarava. A Portuguese translation of *On Old Age* was printed in 1538.

Cicero was known to have written a *Consolatio* to himself for the death of his daughter Tullia and a protreptic work called the *Hortensius*, which famously helped lead St. Augustine to Christianity. The historian Carlo Sigonio composed and circulated under Cicero's name a forged *Consolatio* in 1583, while Jacopo Sadoleto tried to fill the gap caused by the loss of the *Hortensius* with his own *De laudibus philosophiae* of 1538 (McCuaig 1989). A first attempt to collect the fragments of *On the Commonwealth* was made by Pier Vettori in the fourth volume of Robert Estienne's edition (1538) of Cicero's

Opera omnia. A complete collection of Ciceronian fragments was attempted by Carlo Signonio in 1559; subsequent editions by Denys Lambin and others continued to enlarge the collection.

Renaissance commentaries on Cicero's *philosophica* have not been adequately studied by modern scholarship, particularly those preserved only in manuscript. Many of the numerous Renaissance commentaries on Cicero consist simply of philological notes (such as those of Erasmus, Melanchthon, Pier Vettori, Denys Lambin, Paolo Manuzio, Fulvio Orsini) but some amount to full commentaries, often philosophical in character. The principle printed commentaries are the following:

Academica: Omer Talon (1547), Adrien Turnèbe (1553), Johann Rosa (1571).

The Dream of Scipio (from *Republic VI*): Juan Ludovico Vives (1521/23), Petrus Johannes Olivarius (*scholia*, 1538), Petrus Ramus (*praelectiones*, 1546), Gerardus Vossius (1575), Hieronymus Wolf (1584).

On Duties: Pietro Marsi (1481), Omnebono Leoniceno (1481/82), Josse Bade (1499/1500), Francesco Maturanzio (1506), Veit Amerbach (1538), Joachim Camerarius (1538), Conradus Clauser (*analysis*, 1558), Joannes Rivius (*schematismoi*, 1561), Christophorus Corner (*praelectiones*, 1562), Georgius Cracovius (Book I, 1562), Hieronymus Wolf (1563), Raphael Cyllenius Angelus (*oratio ante interpretationem*, 1565), Hieronymus Wolf (*quaestiones*, 1579), Johannes Piscator, "suited to Ramus' teachings" (1582), Martinus Henricus (1582), Joachim Camerarius (*prolegomena*, 1584), Thomas Brasbrigius (*quaestiones*, 1586), Johannes Bentzius (*erotemata*, 1589), Bernhard Cop (1590), Georgius Fabricius (*Idea and method of the "On Duties"*, 1592), Johannes Martini (*tabulae*, 1599), Alexander Scot (1609), Johannes Aeschartus (*anatome* of Book I, 1612).

On Fate: Giorgio Valla (1485), Petrus Ramus (*praelectiones*, 1550), Achilles Statius (1551), Adrien Turnèbe (1552), Salomon Gesner (1594).

On Friendship: Omnibono Leoniceno (1481/82), Josse Bade (1507), Hieronymus Wolf (1584), Joachim Camerarius (*prolegomena*, 1584), Federicus Cerutus (1587).

On Laws: Adrien Turnèbe (1552), Petrus Ramus (*praelectiones*, 1554).

On Old Age: Martino Filetico (1481/82), Josse Bade (1502), Johannes Murmellius (1505), Hieronymus Wolf (1584).

On the Nature of the Gods: Sixt Birck (1545), Matthäus Dresser (1572).

On the Ultimate Ends of Goods and Evils: Pedro Juan Oliver (1536), Johann Rosa (1571).

The Paradoxes of the Stoics: Johannes Gabriel Senensis (1492), Josse Bade (1499), Francesco Maturanzio (1506), Sixt Birck (1545), Omer Talon (1551), Hieronymus Wolf (1584), Joachim Camerarius (*prolegomena*, 1584).

Timaeus (*De universitate*): Giorgio Valla (1485), Joachim Périon (1540).

Topics: Giorgio Valla (1485), Melanchthon (1533), Johannes Visorius (1536), Bartolomeus Latomus (*enarrationes*, 1538), Antonius Goveanus (1545), Omer Talon (*praelectiones*, 1550), Sebastian Fox Morzillo (1550), Caelius Secundus Curio (1553), Antonius Riccobonus (1567).

Tusculan Disputations: Filippo Beroaldo (1496), Georgio Valla (1502), Joachim Camerarius (I:1538; II-V:1543), Johannes Sturm and Johann Lobart Boruss (I:1575), Hieronymus Wolf (*aphorismi, cum explicatione*, 1580).

An attack on Cicero's academic skepticism from the point of view of Aristotle was composed in 1558 by Julius Castellanius which surveys the epistemological doctrines of the ancient schools.[11]

B. Pyrrhonian Skepticism and Sextus Empiricus

A more radical skeptical position than that found in Plato's Academy was advocated by Pyrrho of Elis (ca. 365-275 BC) and his student Timon of Phlius (ca. 320-230 BC). Most of what we know of both philosophers is preserved in Diogenes Laertius and in the works of Sextus Empiricus. The early skeptics seem to have had no followers until Pyrrhonianism was revived by Aenesidemus at the end of the first century BC in a still more radical form. Our evidence of this second phase of Pyrrhonian skepticism comes almost entirely from Sextus.

Sextus Empiricus (ca. 160-210 AD), a medical doctor, left two works which have survived, the *Outlines of Pyrrhonism* in three books and *Against the Professors* in eleven books. The latter is in reality two separate works, *Against the Professors* (I-VI) and *Against the Dogmatists* (VII-XI). The former is a critique of various disciplines including grammar, rhetoric, mathematics, astrology and music; the latter is directed against dogmatic philosophy.

Both works were practically unknown in the Middle Ages. We know of a complete Latin translation of the *Outlines* which survives in three manuscripts of the thirteenth and early fourteenth centuries. But Sextus gradually became well known to Renaissance readers (Schmitt 1983b). Giovanni Lorenzi (ca. 1440-1501) translated a portion of *Against the Professors* I-IV, probably soon after 1485, which survives in two manuscripts, and John Wolley (ca. 1530-1596) translated *Against the Professors* VII, which survives in a single manu-

---

[11] *Adversus M. Tullii Ciceronis Academicas quaestiones disputatio, qua omnium pene philosophorum opinio de percipienda veritate comprehenditur et Aristotelis prae omnibus celebratur philosophia*, Bologna 1558 (Risse 1998, 1:82).

script. A Greek manuscript of the text was in the possession of Francesco Filelfo in 1427. Humanists who cite Sextus Empiricus before the *editio princeps* include Angelo Poliziano, whose 1488 lectures in Florence included excerpts, Gianfrancesco Pico della Mirandola in his *Examen vanitatis gentilium philosophorum* (1495), and Giovanni Pico della Mirandola, particularly in his posthumous *Adversus Astrologiam*. Conrad Gesner published an entry on him in his famous *Bibliotheca* (1545 and many later editions). Another manuscript translation by the Spanish humanist Paéz de Castro was completed some time after 1549. The first Latin translation of the *Outlines* to be printed was that of Henri II Estienne, the scholarly printer (1562). Estienne also oversaw the printing of Gentian Hervet's translation of the *Adversus Mathematicos*, which appeared in 1569. The first Greek edition was not published until 1621, and contained both of Sextus' works, accompanied by a Latin translation and testimonia. As far as is known, there were no vernacular translations and no commentaries on either text made during the Renaissance (Floridi 2002).

IX

NEOPYTHAGOREANS

Pythagoras (ca. 570-ca. 490 BC; see BIOGRAPHY) and his follower Philolaus (ca. 470-ca. 385 BC) are usually included among the PRESOCRATICS, but Neopythagorean revivals began already in the fourth century BC among Plato's followers. The most important revival occurred in Alexandria and Rome in the first century BC and continued down to the end of antiquity; it had close relations with MIDDLE PLATONISM in the first and second centuries AD, and from the time of IAMBLICHUS was absorbed into Neoplatonism. The Pythagoreanism known to the Middle Ages and Renaissance was essentially that of this Neopythagorean movement of the Roman Empire, though testimonia to early Pythagoreanism were to be found in PLATO and ARISTOTLE. Most of what the Renaissance thought it knew about Pythagoreanism came from Censorinus, DIOGENES LAERTIUS, Philostratus' *Life of Apollonius of Tyana* (see BIOGRAPHY), IAMBLICHUS and the Pythagorean pseudoepigrapha anthologized in Stobaeus and other sources (see DOXOGRAPHIES AND ANTHOLOGIES). The most important of these are the *Golden Sayings* and *Symbols* of Pseudo-Pythagoras, Pseudo-Timaeus of Locri's *On the Soul and the Cosmos* (a Hellenistic forgery purporting to be the source of Plato's *Timaeus*), and Pseudo-Ocellus Lucanus' *On the Nature of the Universe* (based in part on Aristotle's *On Generation and Corruption*). Numerous fragments also survive of Philolaus, some of which are still thought genuine, and of Archytas of Tarentum, a Pythagorean contemporary of Plato. Archytas' fragments are now regarded as forgeries. A collection of forged letters of Pythagoras and his school also circulated. A commentary on the *Golden Sayings* was composed by the Neoplatonist HIEROCLES OF ALEXANDRIA (d. 431/ 432 AD), and IAMBLICHUS gave explanations of 39 of the *Symbols* in his *Protrepticus*. BOETHIUS' treatises on arithmetic and music preserved the teaching of the Neopythagorean Nicomachus of Gerasa (second century AD), works which present Pythagoras as the founder of the *quadrivium* (arithmetic, geometry, music, astronomy) and the discoverer of the "music of the spheres". A collection of 451 gnomic utterances circulated under the name of Pope Sixtus (or Xystus) II, which was more plausibly attributed to Sextus the Pythagorean by Jerome. A translation of it was made in antiquity by Rufinus which was first printed in Fano in 1502. For a collection of Neopythagorean sources see Thesleff 1965.

Renaissance Pythagoreanism is relatively unexplored, though for the fifteenth century one may consult Allen 1994 and Celenza 2001, and for Pythagorean influences in poetry there is Heninger 1974. The first Renaissance humanist to take a serious interest in Pythagorean texts was the Sicilian Giovanni Aurispa (1376-1459), who brought works of Iamblichus back from the Greek East and translated HIEROCLES' commentary on the *Golden Sayings* in 1449. One of Ficino's mentors, Antonio degli Agli (d. 1477), composed a commentary on the *Symbols*, as did Filippo Beroaldo (ca. 1480), Giovanni Nesi – a student of Ficino who became a follower of Savonarola (1500) –, and Lilio Gregorio Giraldi (written 1507, printed 1551), who was a follower of Gianfrancesco Pico. Ficino himself translated both the *Golden Sayings* and the *Symbols* (both published in 1497); the Greek text of the former had been published the year before by Aldus. The *Golden Sayings* became a popular schooltext, and other versions were made by Caspar Ursinus Velius (1524), Veit Amerbach (1539), Gerhard Mathisius (1553), Michael Neander (1559), among others, and school commentaries were composed by Amerbach (1539), Stefano Negri (1550), Théodore Marcile (1585) and Wolfgang Seberus (1622). There were at least two more commentaries on the *Symbols* published in the sixteenth century, those by Joannes Alexander Brassicanus (1532) and Pomponius Brunellus (1597). Pseudo-Timaeus Locrus was translated by Gregorio Tifernate in 1457 (Hankins 1990), but the most popular version was that made by Giorgio Valla, printed in 1498. The *editio princeps* of the Greek was published in the Aldine Plato of 1513; a new edition and Latin translation was made by Ludovico Nogarola in 1555. Rufinus' translation of Sextus Pythagoreus was first printed in 1502. A Latin translation of Pseudo-Ocellus was published by Joannnes Boscius in 1554, and the *Letters of the Pythagoreans* were printed in 1598. Nicomachus of Gerasa's two surviving works, an *Introduction to Arithmetic* and *Manual of Harmonics* were first printed in 1538 and 1616 respectively; Joachim Camerarius published notes to the former text in 1554. From the time of Copernicus Pythagoras was cited as ancient authority for a heliocentric cosmos on the basis of comments in various patristic authorities (Campanella 2006). Pythagoras' putative support for heliocentrism was invoked by Galileo, Bruno and Campanella among others.

An anonymous French translation of the *Golden Sayings* was published in Lyon in 1596.

Attempts were made to collect the fragments of the ancient Pythagorean writers as early as 1570 by Willem Canter, who published a Greek text and translation of the Pythagorean fragments preserved in Stobaeus as an appendix to the Stephanus edition of Diogenes Laertius. Estienne also published a collection of the fragments of Archytas in an edition of Aristotle and Theophrastus (1557). These collections of Pythagorean fragments were extremely popular and were continuously enlarged; the most important late Renaissance collection was that of Joachim Zehner (1603).

X

NEOPLATONISTS

Neoplatonism is generally considered a phase of Platonism initiated by PLOTINUS in the third century AD and continued by PORPHYRY, IAMBLICHUS, PROCLUS and others. It lasted in its pagan form into the sixth century and influenced many early Christian and Muslim authors. The figures most important for the Renaissance are given below; see also the COMMENTATORS on PLATO and ARISTOTLE for Neoplatonist commentary literature and NEOPYTHAGOREANISM.

A. PLOTINUS

Plotinus (204-270 AD) was the most important Neoplatonic philosopher. His various essays were collected by his pupil PORPHYRY into six groups of nine essays, the *Enneads*. These were published around the years 300-305 with Porphyry's biography of Plotinus. Some part of these were translated into Latin by Marius Victorinus in the fourth century and were almost certainly known to Augustine, but the translation does not survive. Plotinus was also known indirectly via various later Neoplatonic and early Christian writers. His works were unknown in the medieval Latin West.

Interest in his writings was eventually stimulated by Pletho and Bessarion in the fifteenth century. Ficino began a translation in 1484 of the *Enneads* which was published in 1492, reprinted in 1540, and reprinted in revised form in 1559, 1562, 1580 and 1615. Plotinus is often cited in Ficino's other works and was a major influence on his philosophy. The Greek text of Plotinus was not printed until 1580, when it appeared in parallel columns with Ficino's translation. This was the last Greek edition before the nineteenth century. In the sixteenth century an Arabic compilation based on *Enneads IV-VI*, the so-called *Theology of Aristotle*, was translated into Latin in 1519 (see PSEUDO-

ARISTOTLE). The only major Renaissance commentary is that of Ficino, published with his 1492 translation and with all five sixteenth-century reprints. It was also reprinted without the translation in the three sixteenth century editions of Ficino's *Opera omnia*, the first of which appeared in 1561 (O'Meara 1992).

B. PORPHYRY

Plotinus' student Porphyry (234-ca. 305 AD) is credited with at least sixty-nine works, including (a) commentaries on Aristotle and an introduction (*Isagoge*) to his logical writings; (b) commentaries on Plato, including extensive fragments of a commentary on the *Timaeus*; (c) his edition of Plotinus with a lost commentary, plus the *Sententiae ad intelligibilia ducentes*, an introduction to Plotinian metaphysics; (d) lives of Pythagoras and Plotinus (see BIOGRAPHY); (e) an attack on Christianity, preserved in fragmentary form in Origen's reply; (f) other writings on religion, including a treatise on vegetarianism (*On Abstinence*), *On Statues*, *Philosophy from Oracles* (of which there are extensive citations in Eusebius' *Preparation for the Gospel*), *The Return of the Soul* (numerous citations in Augustine's *City of God*); and a pair of philosophical letters. He also composed works of literary scholarship and works on technical scientific subjects which will not be discussed here. Origen, Eusebius, Augustine, Macrobius and PROCLUS are important indirect sources (Porphyry 1993). There is a brief biography of Porphyry by Eunapius (see BIOGRAPHY).

Of these works by far the best known in the Middle Ages and Renaissance was the *Isagoge*, which was translated by BOETHIUS and became the standard introduction to ARISTOTLE's *Organon* in the Latin scholastic world. Over three hundred manuscripts and innumerable printed editions survive of this Latin translation; the first printing was 1473. The first Greek edition was printed with the Aldine Aristotle in 1495. John Argyropoulos made a new Latin translation which was first printed in 1496, but it failed to replace Boethius'. Giovanni Bernardo Feliciano's translation of 1548 also failed to catch on. In the sixteenth century, Boethius' translation continues to account for more than half of the editions, though Perionius' translation became popular in the second half of the century (Cranz and Schmitt 1984). There were many scholastic commentaries on the *Isagoge*, of which Duns Scotus' and John Buridan's were among the most widely circulated (Lohr 1967-74). AMMONIUS' commentary was first printed in Greek in 1500 and first became available in Latin in 1526.

The other philosophical works were much less known. Ficino translated the *Life of Plotinus* for his Plotinus edition of 1492, and this was included in all the reprints. He also translated the *Sententiae* and passages from *On Abstinence* which were published in a famous Aldine collection of Platonica (1497) that was reprinted six times by different publishers. The Greek text of *On Abstinence* and the *Sententiae* was edited by Pier Vettori in an imprint of 1548. A year earlier a Latin translation of *On Abstinence* had been published by Giovanni Bernardino Feliciano. A bilingual volume containing the *Sententiae* and *On Abstinence*, edited and translated with notes by François de Fourgerolles, appeared in 1620. The *editio princeps* of the *Life of Pythagoras*, edited by Konrad Rittershausen, was published in 1610, accompanied by notes of Daniel Heinsius. The first serious study of Porphyry's works was contained in a bilingual Latin and Greek edition edited by Lucas Holstenius in 1630, which included the *Life of Pythagoras*, the *Sententiae*, Porphyry's study of *Odyssey XIII* (*The Cave of the Nymphs*), and Holstenius' *Dissertatio de vita et scriptis Porphyrii et ad vitam Pythagorae observationes*, which contained among much else a discussion of Porphyry's *Contra Christianos*.

C. Iamblichus

Iamblichus (ca. 245-ca. 325 AD) of Chalcis studied with Porphyry but founded his own Neoplatonic school which emphasized Platonism's links with Pythagoreanism and other ancient theologies as well as mathematics, theurgy and ritual. His extant works include a collection of works on Pythagoreanism (*The Pythagorean Life*, *Protrepticus*, *On General Mathematical Science* and *On Nicomachus' Introduction to Arithmetic*). Also preserved is *On the Mysteries*, an attempt to give Neoplatonic theurgy a philosophical basis. Stobaeus (see Doxographies and Anthologies) also preserves extensive fragments of *On the Soul* and some letters. A work called *Theological Principles of Arithmetic* has been dubiously attributed to Iamblichus in modern times; the work was published in an anonymous Latin translation in 1543.

The most important source for Iamblichus' thought in the Renaissance was Ficino's translation of *On the Mysteries*, made in 1488 and published by Aldus in 1497 (Kristeller 1938). This collection of Platonica was reprinted by various publishers six times, the last edition being published in 1607. Ficino's version of *On the Mysteries* was also reprinted in another Platonic collection in 1532. A literal translation of the same text was made by Nicolaus Scutellius of Trent and published in 1556 along with Scutellius' translation of *The Py-*

thagorean Life (see BIOGRAPHY). *The Pythagorean Life* and the *Protrepticus* were edited in Greek for the first time in 1598 with a Latin translation by Johannes Arcerius Theodoretus of Frisia. A translation of *The Pythagorean Life* was prepared by Lucas Holstenius but never published (Iamblichus 1975). The standard version of Pythagoras' *Symbols*, reprinted a number of times, was taken from Iamblichus' *Protrepticus* (see NEOPYTHAGOREANS). The *editiones principes* of *On Nicomachus' Introduction to Arithmetic* and *On the Mysteries* had to wait until 1668 and 1678 respectively.

D. JULIAN ("THE APOSTATE")

The Roman emperor Flavius Claudius Julianus (331-363 AD), called "the Apostate" by his Christian enemies, was a follower of Iamblichan Neoplatonism though he also studied with the Aristotelian commentator Themistius. Of his surviving works, *Orations* IV-VIII are philosophical in character and discuss the theology and theurgy of the Neoplatonists (IV-V) and critique contemporary Cynicism (VI-VII), while a number of the letters are addressed to contemporary philosophers and discuss philosophical issues. The orations were never printed or translated during the Renaissance, though a Greek copy of *Oration IV*, to "King Helios", was annotated by Ficino (*Iter* 1:184). The *editio princeps* of the letters, with a Latin translation, was published by Petrus Martinius of Navarre in 1566; *Oration IV* was published in 1625 in a Latin translation by Vincentius Marinerius. An edition of the complete works in Greek and Latin was published by Denys Pétau in 1630.

E. SALLUSTIUS

The pagan philosopher Sallustius or Salustius or Salutius (fourth century AD), a friend of Julian, was the author of *On the Gods and the World*, "a little catechism of popular Neoplatonism" (Bowersock 1978). A manuscript copy was owned by the bibliophile Gian Vincenzo Pinelli (1535-1601). It was first edited and translated by Leone Allacci, the prefect of the Vatican Library, who published it in Rome in 1638 with a preface by Gabriel Naudé, the free-thinking librarian of the Bibliothèque Mazarine, and notes by the great scholar of ancient Platonism, Lucas Holstenius. A duplicate edition appeared the next year in Leiden (Sallustius 1960).

F. Hierocles of Alexandria

Hierocles of Alexandria (d. 431/32) wrote a commentary on the *Golden Verses* of Pseudo-Pythagoras (see Neopythagoreans). This was first translated into Latin by Giovanni Aurispa in 1449, whose version was published in 1474 and often reprinted. The first Greek edition appeared in 1583, edited and translated by Joannes Curterius. A French translation by Gulielmus Rheginus was printed in 1560, an Italian translation by Dardi Bembo in 1604, and an English translation by John Hall in 1655.

Hierocles also wrote a treatise *On Providence*, whose *editio princeps* appeared in 1597 with a translation by Fédéric Morel (the translation alone was first published in 1593). Hugo Grotius prepared a compendium based on Hierocles' treatise which was published in 1648 in his *De fato*.

There are also fragments from an ethical handbook of Hierocles the Stoic (second century AD) in Stobaeus and Eusebius which were mistakenly attributed to Hierocles of Alexandria in Meric Casaubon's edition of 1655.

G. Macrobius

Ambrosius Theodosius Macrobius (fl. 430 AD) wrote in Latin a *Commentary on the Dream of Scipio*, a long passage from Book VI of Cicero's *On the Commonwealth*. The work draws heavily on Porphyry's commentary on Plato's *Timaeus*, which survives only in fragments. Manuscripts of Macrobius' work were widely diffused in the Latin Middle Ages. The text was a favorite of twelfth-century Platonists and numerous glossary commentaries are preserved (Munk Olsen 1982). The *editio princeps* was printed by Nicolaus Jenson in 1472, and at least four more editions of the work appeared before 1500. It was published at least 27 times in the sixteenth century.

H. Proclus

Next to Plotinus, Proclus (ca. 410-485 AD) is our most important surviving source for Neoplatonic philosophy. In addition to his commentaries on Plato (see Plato, Commentators) he composed a number of independent philosophical works, including *Elements of Theology*, *Platonic Theology*, *Elements of Physics*, and three short treatises *On Providence*, *On Providence and*

Fate, On the Subsistence of Evil. Two works on pagan religion circulate under his name as well, *On Sacrifice and Magic* and *Extracts on Chaldaean Philosophy*. He also composed a number of technical scientific and literary works which will not be discussed in this entry. A life of Proclus was written by his student Marinus (see BIOGRAPHY). Proclus was known directly in the Middle Ages thanks to William of Moerbeke, who translated *Elements of Theology* (1268), the commentary on the *Parmenides* (undated), extracts of the *Timaeus* commentary (before 1274) and the so-called *Tria opuscula* (1280), i.e., *On Providence, On Providence and Fate, On the Subsistence of Evil* (Brams and Vanhamel 1989). None of these translations by Moerbeke were printed before modern times. Proclus' philosophy was also known indirectly to the medieval Latin West via PSEUDO-DIONYSIUS THE AREOPAGITE and the PSEUDO-ARISTOTLE'S *Liber de causis*. The latter was based on an Arabic version of the *Elements of Theology*. Aquinas was the first to identify it as a work of Proclus, thanks to Moerbeke's translation of the *Elements*, though the work continued to circulate under Aristotle's name down to the sixteenth century and was the object of numerous commentaries by Latin scholastics. The *Elements of Theology* was particularly influential among the Rhenish followers of Albert the Great, and Berthold von Moosburg composed a commentary on it which was published only in the twentieth century (de Libera 1984; von Moosburg 1974-84).

Proclus became somewhat better known in the Renaissance, though none of Moerbeke's translations saw print. Cusanus drew heavily on the medieval translation of the *Elements of Theology* and the *Parmenides* commentary, and it was Cusanus who brought the manuscript of the *Platonic Theology* back to Italy from Constantinople. Pietro Balbi, a member of Bessarion's circle, translated it into Latin, a version surviving in three manuscripts. The systematic exposition of Platonism in Book II of Bessarion's *In Calumniatorem Platonis* (1469) owes much to Proclus' *Theology*. Ficino knew his works well, and modelled his own *Platonic Theology* partly on Proclus (Hankins 1990), while Pico della Mirandola drew 65 of his *900 Theses* from Proclus.

Ficino translated the short treatise *On Sacrifice and Magic* in 1488 which was published in the Aldine collection of Platonica in 1497 and reprinted six times by various printers; it was also included in another collection of Ficino's Platonica printed in 1532. The first Greek edition of the *Platonic Theology* and *Elements of Theology* was that of Aemilius Portus of 1618, who also supplied his own Latin translation. A *Compendiaria de motu disputatio* from an unidentified source was published by Simon Grynaeus as a work of Proclus in 1531, and a Latin translation of the text was printed in 1542. Francesco Patrizi published Latin translations of the *Elements of Theology* and *Elements of Physics*

5

in 1583. By far the most popular work associated with Proclus' name is the spurious astronomical treatise *On the Sphere*, which circulated in innumerable editions and was translated into English, French and Italian during the Renaissance; commentaries were composed on the text by Joannes Stoefler (1534) and Georgius Henischius (1609).

I. DAMASCIUS

See PLATO, COMMENTATORS. Damascius' *De principiis* survived in a single Greek manuscript. This made its way into the library of Cardinal Bessarion in the fifteenth century, who corrected and annotated it. About 30 manuscripts were copied from Bessarion's manuscript directly or indirectly between the fifteenth and seventeenth century, including copies owned by William Grocyn, Francesco Patrizi, Lucas Holstenius, and Nicholas Peiresc. There were no editions of the Greek text and no Latin translations of the work in the Renaissance. The text was first printed in 1826, though excerpts were published in 1724 by Johann Christian Wolf in his *Anecdota Graeca* (Damascius 1986-91). For Damascius' *Life of Isidore* see BIOGRAPHY.

J. PSEUDO-DIONYSIUS THE AREOPAGITE

Pseudo-Dionysius was a Christian Neoplatonist, probably a Syrian Monophysite (fl. ca. 485-528), who falsely represented himself in his works as the Athenian judge converted by the Apostle Paul in the book of Acts (17:34). Under this disguise he wrote four treatises and ten letters which present Christian versions of the philosophy of Proclus, with whom he probably studied. The corpus of Pseudo-Dionysius includes *Divine Names*, *Mystical Theology*, *Celestial Hierarchy* and *Ecclesiastical Hierarchy*, plus the ten letters; many Renaissance editions contain an eleventh letter, which is a medieval Latin forgery based on the seventh letter.

Though Dionysius' authorship was suspected as early as the sixth century in Byzantium, his works nevertheless acquired quasi-apostolic authority in the Latin West during the Middle Ages. The works of Pseudo-Dionysius were widely available in Western Christendom after the first Latin translations were made by Hilduin and John Scotus Eriugena in the ninth century. John the Saracen and Grosseteste produced a fresh translations of the entire corpus in the twelfth and thirteenth centuries respectively. His theology exerted a profound influence on major medieval theologians, including Eriugena himself, Hugh of St. Victor, Robert Grosseteste, Albert the Great, Bonaventure, Aquinas and Meister Eckhardt. Eriugena, Hugh, Grosseteste, Thomas Gallus, Albert and Aquinas all composed commentaries on Dionysian texts. The medieval versions and commentaries were well known to Nicholas of Cusa, upon whom they had a formative influence. Dionysian authorship of the treatises was first seriously questioned in the West during the 1440s and 1450s by Theodore Gaza and Lorenzo Valla, and doubts spread rapidly after Erasmus lent his authority to them after 1504 (Monfasani 1987). Luther, Calvin and most Protestants rejected the authenticity of Dionysius' writings, while they continued to be accepted by some Catholic theologians well into the seventeenth century.

In the Renaissance the four treatises and the letters were translated anew by the humanist monk Ambrogio Traversari (1436/1437), a version which circulated widely in manuscript before being printed in 1498 in an edition prepared by Jacques Lefèvre d'Etaples. This was the most popular Renaissance version, reprinted at least seven times before being supplanted by the new version of Joachim Périon, first published in 1556. Ficino translated the *Mystical Theology* in 1491 and the *Divine Names* in 1492, both with commentary; these works were first published in Venice in 1496 and at least five times thereafter. The medieval translations of John the Saracen and Grosseteste with a selection of medieval commentaries were printed in an important, three-volume omnibus edition of 1502-03, along with Traversari's and Ficino's versions. The translations of Eriugena and John the Saracen were printed in 1536 and 1556, together with the versions of Traversari and Ficino. John the Saracen's translation of the *Mystical Theology* was also reprinted with Ficino's translation and a commentary by Luther's Dominican critic, Johannes Eck, in 1519.

In addition to Ficino's and Eck's commentaries, Denys of Ryckel (Dionysius Cartusiensis, 1402-71) composed commentaries on all the treatises, published in 1536 and 1556, and Périon's translations also included *scholia*, though these are of limited philosophical interest. John Colet (1467-1519), an English disciple of Ficino, wrote two treatises on Dionysius' *Celestial* and *Ecclesiastical Hierarchy* which were not published, however, until 1869. George Pachymeres' paraphrase of Dionysius' works was first published in Greek in 1561. The first Greek edition of all four treatises and the letters was published in Florence in 1516. A French translation by Jean Goulu was printed in 1608; it is the only known vernacular version of the Renaissance (Dionysius the Areopagite [Pseudo] 1937-50).

K. JOHN PHILOPONUS

See ARISTOTLE, COMMENTATORS. In addition to his Aristotle commentaries, his grammatical, mathematical and specialized theological works and a treatise on the astrolabe, Philoponus also wrote philosophical treatises *On the Eternity of the World against Proclus* (529 AD), which defends a creationist interpretation of the *Timaeus*; *On the Eternity of the World Against Aristotle* (ca. 530-534 AD), another defense of creationism which survives only in fragments; and *On the Creation of the World* (ca. 546-549 AD), a theological work which proposes a theory of impetus (Scholten 1996, 429-435).

Though known prior to the sixteenth century via manuscripts held in Rome, Venice and Florence, the treatise against Proclus was first printed in Greek in 1535. Latin translations were published by Gaspar Marcellus Montagnensis in 1551 and Jean Mahot in 1557 (Schmitt 1989). The theological treatise on the creation of the world was first published in Greek in 1630 with a Latin translation by Balthasar Corderius. The fragments of the treatise on eternity against Aristotle were not assembled until the twentieth century. For the life of Aristotle attributed to Philoponus, now assigned to Ammonius, see BIOGRAPHY.

L. BOETHIUS

The philosophical works of Anicius Manlius Severinus Boethius (ca. 480-524 AD) were well known to the Latin scholastics of the Middle Ages and continued to be widely studied in the Renaissance. The *editio princeps* of the *Consolation of Philosophy* was 1464 and the work continued to be reprinted with great regularity, often with Pseudo-Aquinas' commentary; it was translated into all the major Western vernaculars, usually from very early dates. For example, the work was translated into Anglo-Saxon by King Alfred and into Middle English verse by Chaucer. The text was often read in schools and many glossed copies survive from the Renaissance (Black and Pomaro 2000). Printed commentaries were composed by Josse Bade (1503), Raymundus Palasinus (1515), and Johannes Murmellius (1516), among others; Denys the Carthusian's fifteenth century commentary was printed in 1540. For Boethius' translations of philosophical texts see ARISTOTLE and PORPHYRY; for his commentary on Cicero's *Topics* see CICERO.

M. ANONYMOUS, *PROLEGOMENON TO PLATONIC PHILOSOPHY*

This work is assigned tentatively to the Alexandrian school of Platonism and the second half of the sixth century by L. G. Westerink. It survives in a single manuscript now in Vienna, formerly in the collection of the Hungarian physician and humanist Janus Sambucus (1531-84). There is no evidence that it was known to the Italian Platonists of the fifteenth century (Anonymous 1962).

XI

BIOGRAPHY

A. DIOGENES LAERTIUS

The most importance source of biographical information on ancient philosophers for the Renaissance was Diogenes Laertius (early third century AD) whose *Lives of Eminent Philosophers*, written in Greek, contained eighty-two short lives of philosophers from all schools and information about many other philosophers who were not explicitly the subject of a separate biography.

A translation, now lost, was made by Henricus Aristippus in the twelfth century; it does not seem to have had much circulation but became the basis of the popular compendium *On the Lives and Mores of the Philosophers* (before 1326), widely (though incorrectly) attributed to Walter Burley but more probably the work of an Italian author (Grignaschi 1990). Early printers often confused this compendium with the *Lives* of Diogenes Laertius himself. Pseudo-Burley's compendium survives in over 270 manuscripts; it was printed eleven times in the fifteenth century (earliest 1470) and seven times in the sixteenth (latest 1530), before being replaced by translations of Diogenes Laertius himself. Pseudo-Burley was translated into Italian in the fourteenth century and printed in Italian in 1480 and 1535. There was also a Spanish translation of the Pseudo-Burley text, made in the fifteenth century by Hernando Díaz de Valdepeñas, which was printed in 1527 and 1541 (Burley 2002). An anonymous German translation was printed in 1490 and reprinted in 1519.

The first surviving Latin translation of Diogenes Laertius himself was completed about 1433 by the Camaldolese monk Ambrogio Traversari at the request of Cosimo de' Medici, from a Greek manuscript brought back from the east in the 1420s by Giovanni Aurispa (Gigante 1988). Traversari's translation circulated widely in manuscript (it was used extensively by Ficino, among others) and was first printed in Rome ca. 1472. It was reprinted at least 22 times before 1600, though it was revised by various scholars including Joannes Boulierius, Janus Sambucus and Henricus Stephanus. A new translation by

Thomas Aldobrandinus (completed in the 1560s and published in 1594) failed to replace the revised Traversari version, which continued to be reprinted into the seventeenth century.

The Greek original did not see print in any form until the biographies of Aristotle and Theophrastus were included in the second volume of Aldus Manutius' Greek Aristotle (1497); the life of Xenophon was published in the Juntine Xenophon of 1527. The first edition of the complete Greek text was printed by Froben in 1533; the standard edition for early modern Europe was that of Henri II Estienne, published in 1570, reprinted in 1593 with Isaac Casaubon's notes.

Annotations on the first nine books were prepared by Thomas Aldobrandinus in the 1560s and printed in the edition of Diogenes overseen by his nephew, Cardinal Aldobrandini, published in 1594. Stephanus' notes in his 1570 edition were enlarged by Isaac Casaubon for the 1593 edition; an edition of 1664 collected the notes of Aldobrandini, Estienne, Isaac and Meric Casaubon, and Gilles Ménage, most of which are philological in character. Isaac Hortibonus composed notes on the *Lives*, published in Geneva in 1583. Pierre Gassendi's *Animadversiones* on the life of Epicurus (Book X) were published in Leiden in 1649 as a pendant to his *Life and Mores of Epicurus* of 1647. The Scottish humanist Walter Donaldson constructed an account of the rise and progress of philosophy out of Diogenes Laertius in 1625 entitled *Electa Laërtiana*.

An Italian translation was made by Bartolomeo, Lodovico and Pietro Rositini that was first published in 1545; an Italian paraphrase based on Diogenes and other sources was published by Giosefo Salviati in 1598. A French version by François de Fougerolles appeared in 1602.

B. OTHER BIOGRAPHICAL SOURCES

1. *Biographical Compendia*

In addition to Diogenes Laertius, there were several other biographical compendia containing information about philosophers known in the Renaissance. Philostratus' *Lives of the Sophists* (third century AD) was first published in Greek by Aldus in 1502; the first Latin version was by Antonio Bonfini (d. 1502), printed in 1516. A French version by Blaise de Vigenère was published in 1599. Eunapius' *Lives of the Sophists* (ca. 396 AD), by a Neoplatonic opponent of Christianity, deals mostly with fourth-century

Neoplatonists. The first edition in Greek appeared in 1568 with a Latin translation by Adriaan de Jonge (Hadrianus Junius); it was dedicated to Queen Elizabeth I of England. An English translation of the work followed in 1579. The sixth-century *Lives of Men Famous for Learning* attributed to Hesychius of Miletus, known from the Souda, was published by Adriaan de Jonge in a Greek-Latin edition of 1572. A new edition was published by Stephanus in 1593, and a new edition with a new Latin translation by Johannes van Meurs (Meursius) in 1613.

2. *Individual Biographies*

Apollonius of Tyana: Philostratus' life of this Pythagorean holy man was cited by Ficino in his *Platonic Theology* (1469-74; published 1482) and was translated into Latin by the Florentine Alamanno Rinuccini (1419-99). Rinuccini's translation was published in 1501, as revised by Filippo Beroaldo; the Greek was first published by Aldus in 1502. Three separate Italian translations appeared in the same year, 1549, made by Francesco Baldelli, Ludovico Dolce, and Giovambernardo Gualandi. Apollonius had become an "icon of paganism" after being used by Sossianus Hierocles in an attack on Christianity during the fourth century, and in the Renaissance Philostratus' life was usually printed with Eusebius' *Reply to Hierocles*, translated by Zenobi Acciaiuoli (1502), to serve as an "antidote" (Philostratus 2005, 2006).

ARISTOTLE: For the ancient biographical tradition of Aristotle in the Middle Ages and Renaissance see Düring 1957. The *Vita latina* of Aristotle was first printed in 1482. The first volume of the Aldine Greek Aristotle of 1495 contained, in addition to Diogenes Laertius' life, a life of Aristotle sometimes assigned to AMMONIUS, but attributed there to JOHN PHILOPONUS.

Isidore: DAMASCIUS composed a life of his teacher Isidore which is preserved in Photius' *Bibliotheca*, cod. 181 (Proclus 1900-03). Photius' *Biblioteca* was first published in Greek in 1601 and a Latin translation by Andreas Schottus was published in 1606.

PLATO: 148 classical anecdotes of the life of Plato are collected in Riginos 1976. In addition to DIOGENES LAERTIUS' life and APULEIUS' *De Platone et eius dogmate*, biographical material on Plato could be found in OLYMPIODORUS' commentary on the *First Alcibiades*.

PLOTINUS: PORPHYRY'S *Life of Plotinus* was translated into Latin by Ficino, and printed in the Latin *Enneads* edition of 1492, then at least five times in the sixteenth century, most importantly in the revised version of 1559. It also appeared in *Opera omnia* editions of Ficino's own works. The Greek text appeared for the first time in the 1580 bilingual *Enneads*.

PROCLUS: The life of Proclus by his student Marinus circulated widely in manuscript; copies were owned by Carteromachus, Francesco Patrizi of Cherso and Lucas Holstenius among others. The work was first edited in Greek by Konrad Gesner, with an anonymous Latin translation and *scholia*, in 1559 as a pendant to the *editio princeps* of Marcus Aurelius' *Meditations*; it was published again in the 1618 bilingual *editio princeps* of Proclus' *Platonic Theology* (Marinus 1985).

Pythagoras: Iamblichus' *On the Pythagorean Life* contains much biographical material about Pythagoras (see IAMBLICHUS). See PORPHYRY for his life of Pythagoras. On the authority of St. Ambrose (*CSEL* LXXXII, 39) Pythagoras was widely believed to have been of Jewish origin and to have borrowed much of his philosophy from Moses.

SENECA: Jerome's life of Seneca in his *De viris illustribus*, chapter 12, was well known throughout the Middle Ages and Renaissance; for the three medieval and twelve Renaissance biographies of Seneca see Fohlen 2002.

XII

DOXOGRAPHIES AND ANTHOLOGIES

Several introductory summaries or doxographies of ancient philosophy survived from the ancient world (Diels 1929; Runia 1999; Mansfeld 2004) and were known in the Renaissance. In Latin these were often referred to as *placita* or *opiniones philosophorum*. They contained accounts of a philosopher's doctrines or views, with or without a treatment of the argumentation for those doctrines or views. Aside from those contained or utilized in works of ARISTOTLE, CICERO, PLUTARCH, DIOGENES LAERTIUS and APULEIUS, the most important such texts circulating in the Renaissance were as follows: (a) Pseudo-Plutarch's *On the Teachings of the Philosophers* (included in volume XI of the *Moralia*; see PLUTARCH), most likely an epitome of a lost doxography by Aëtius. (b) Pseudo-Galen's *Research on the History of Philosophy*, an epitome of the same Pseudo-Plutarch text, probably made sometime between the third and fifth century AD. (c) Galen, *Opinions of Hippocrates and Plato*. (b) and (c) were handed down with the corpus of Galen, but the latter was not known in the West before the Renaissance. Pseudo-Plutarch and Stobaeus' *Anthology* (see below) between them preserved most of Aëtius (late first-early second century AD). The close relationship between Pseudo-Plutarch and Pseudo-Galen's *Research* was already observed by Guillaume Budé, who translated the Plutarchan doxography in 1505, but Konrad Gesner was the first to suggest that the two texts should be combined into a single treatise. The *editio princeps* was printed in Basel in 1531 with Budé's translation. In 1571 Francesco Patrizi argued that Pseudo-Galen derived from Pseudo-Plutarch, and was the first to attribute the lost original work to Aëtius, an argument silently followed by Diels and later scholarship (Mansfeld and Runia 1997). (d) Arius Didymus' epitome of physical teaching was preserved primarily in Eusebius' *Praeparatio evangelica*, Stobaeus and ALCINOUS' *Handbook*. (e) Censorinus' *De die natali* (ca. 238 AD) also preserved rich doxographical material (Schmitt, Skinner and Kessler 1988); it was first published in 1497.

Over 630 editions of Galen were published between the invention of printing and 1600, Galen holding a position in medical education analogous to that of Aristotle in philosophy, and these have not been fully explored by modern scholarship. But it appears that the earliest Latin translation of *Research* was that of Niccolò da Reggio (fl. 1308-45), first printed in 1515-16, while the Greek text (under the title *De philosopho historia*) was first published in the Aldine Aristotle of 1497. New Latin translations were later made by Julianus Martianus Rota, first published in 1541-42, and Andrés de Laguna in 1543. Books II-IX only of the *Opinions* were translated by Johannes Guinterius (Winter) in 1534 and by Johannes Bernardus Felicianus (Regazzola) in 1535 (Risse 1998). The first edition and translation of Book I was made by John Caius, published in 1544 (Durling 1961); Janus Cornarius made a fresh Latin translation of all nine books that was published in 1550. Also ascribed to Galen is a *Fragment from Four Commentaries on Medical Passages in Plato's Timaeus*, first translated by Augustus Gadaldinus in Gesner's important edition of Galen of 1549-51. Galen's protreptic, *That a Good Doctor should also be a Philosopher*, was popularized by a translation of Erasmus, first published in 1526.

Doxographies were also excerpted or compiled by various Christian writers, of which the most important are Clement of Alexandria's *Stromateis* (late second century), Hermias' *Mockery of the Heathen Philosophers* (third century?), and Theodoret of Cyrrhus' *Cure for Greek Illnesses* (first half of the fifth century). Clement's *Stromateis* was edited in Greek by Pier Vettori (1550), then translated into Latin by Gentian Hervet (1551). The *editio princeps* of Hermias appeared in 1553, together with a Latin translation by Raphael Seiler (Hermias 1993). Theodoretus' *Cure* was translated into Latin by Zenobi Acciaiuoli and published in 1519; the *editio princeps* had to wait until 1592.

For medieval and Renaissance doxographies see Risse 1998, vol. 7.

Much important material concerning ancient philosophy was also preserved in the anthology by John of Stobi or Stobaeus (fifth century AD), containing many excerpts from ancient writers on physics and ethics. Most of this work was translated into Latin by Camers Varinus in 1517. The *editio princeps* was edited by Vittore Trincavelli in 1536, but the most important sixteenth-century edition was that of Konrad Gesner (1543 and many reprints), which set off a wave of research into the history of philosophy. Another important edition was that of Willem Canter (1575). A Byzantine compilation made by "Suidas" (i.e., the *Souda*, first published in Greek by Aldus in 1514, first complete Latin version in 1619) and Photius' ninth-century *Biblioteca* (first published in 1601) also provided information and testimonia not available in other surviving sources.

XIII

THEOSOPHICAL WRITINGS

A. The Hermetic Corpus

The *Corpus Hermeticum* is a collection of Greek writings from the second or third century AD influenced by Platonism and Gnosticism. It was attributed in antiquity to Hermes Trismegistus (or Mercurius Trismegistus), the legendary "ancient theologian", who was thought to be a contemporary of Moses. Hermes was seen in the Renaissance as the fountainhead of the Egyptian tradition of theology, as Zoroaster was of the Persian and Orpheus of the Greek (representing the three known continents of Africa, Asia and Europe). Apuleius translated a part of the corpus, called *Asclepius*, into Latin (see APULEIUS). Interest in the Hermetic corpus was revived in the fifteenth century by Pletho and Ficino and continued strongly throughout the Renaissance until Isaac Casaubon exposed the Hermetic corpus as the work of a "half-Christian forger" in 1614 (Gentile and Gilly 1999; Hermes Trismegistus [Pseudo] 1992).

The *Pimander* (= *Corpus Hermeticum I-XIV*) was first translated by Ficino in 1463, a version which circulated widely in manuscript and was published in 1471. There were more than two dozen printings of the text by the mid-sixteenth century (Hermes Trismegistus [Pseudo] 1992). A commentary in the form of a synopsis was published by Jacques Lefèvre d'Etaples in his edition of the text (1494). The first translation of the *Definitiones* (= *Corpus Hermeticum XVI*), that of Lodovico Lazzarelli, was made in the late fifteenth century and published in 1507 with a commentary by Symphorien Champier. The first Greek printing of Hermetic texts was a bilingual edition of 1554 prepared by Adrian Turnèbe containing *Corpus Hermeticum* I-XIV, XVI-XVIII and Hermetic excerpts from Stobaeus (see DOXOGRAPHIES AND ANTHOLOGIES). In Foix de Candale's edition of 1574, edited with the help of Joseph Scaliger, the Stobaeus excerpts were combined with a fragment from the Souda (see DOXOGRAPHIES AND ANTHOLOGIES) and numbered as *Corpus*

Hermeticum XV. In his *Nova de universis philosophia* of 1591 Francesco Patrizi also published translations of the *Corpus* following his own ordering system; he was the first to note that *Poimandres* is the name of the first treatise only, not of the entire collection (Hermes Trismegistus [Pseudo] 1924, 1992).

A Latin Hermetic work of the later twelfth century, the *Liber XXIV philosophorum*, circulated in manuscript, and though it was never printed in the Renaissance, it was certainly known to Cusanus (see Moran 2007). The *Liber de VI rerum principiis*, a twelfth-century Latin work ascribed to Mercurius, survived only in a few manuscripts (Dannenfeldt 1960b). Beginning in 1494, Ptolemy's *Centiloquium* was often falsely attributed to Hermes in printed texts. A number of alchemical, iatromathematical, astronomical and divinatory texts were also attributed to Hermes in the Renaissance; see Gilly and van Heertum 2002.

An Italian version of the *Pimander* by Tommaso Benci, supervised by Ficino, was completed in 1463 and published in 1548. Gabriel du Préau's French *Pimandre* was printed in 1549; Foix de Candale's in 1579. German, Dutch and English translations appeared in 1608, 1643 and 1649, respectively.

B. The Orphic Hymns

The mythical singer Orpheus was seen by ancient Neoplatonists and Neopythagoreans as a source of theosophical knowledge and by the Renaissance as the fountainhead of the Greek tradition of "ancient theology", a philosophical ancestor of Pythagoras and Plato. A number of hexameters purportedly written by him were preserved in Neoplatonic authors and the Church Fathers, and a corpus of hymns, mostly revolving around the god Dionysus, is preserved. Ficino translated as lines of Orpheus some verses from the hymns in his *Platonic Theology* (Ficino 2001-06) and there survive two manuscript translations into Latin, neither of which can be identified as Ficino's (Klutstein 1987). The *editio princeps* of the *Hymns* was published by the Juntine Press in 1500, and an anonymous Latin translation was published in 1540. Henri II Estienne (Stephanus) included some *Orphica* in his *Poesis philosophica* (see PRESOCRATICS) and composed philological notes on the hymns. A narrative poem about the Argonauts, the *Argonautica*, and the *Lithica* or *De lapidibus* were also attributed to Orpheus during the Renaissance, but are not of philosophical interest.

C. The Chaldaean Oracles

This collection of oracular statements, mostly written in Greek dactylic hexameters and revealing Neoplatonic, Neopythagorean and Gnostic influences, existed in some form from the second century AD onwards; the Souda and Psellus attribute an ancient work of this name to Julian the Chaldaean and his son, Julian the Theurge. Chaldaean oracles (or *Magika logia*) were often quoted by Neoplatonic authors from the time of Porphyry on, who regarded them as revealed texts. Our fullest record of the *Oracles* as they existed in antiquity is in Michael Psellus' eleventh-century commentary and exposition of Chaldaic doctrines, evidently derived from a lost commentary of Proclus; this was first edited by Johannes Opsopaeus in 1589. Georgios Gemistos, known as Pletho (d. 1452), made the first Renaissance collection, consisting of 34 oracles; he attributed them Zoroaster's disciples, the Magi. Pletho also composed a commentary on them which was closely studied by Ficino and circulated widely in manuscript (Tambrun 2006). From the time of Ficino the *Oracles* were commonly attributed to Zoroaster (or Zarathustra) himself, whom Ficino and his followers regarded as a source of ancient Persian theosophical wisdom. Ficino quoted some of the oracles from Pletho's collection in his *Platonic Theology* (Ficino 2001-06).

The *editio princeps* of the Plethonian *Oracles*, with Pletho's commentary, was published in 1538 (Pletho 1995). The first published Latin translation of the *Oracles* and Pletho's commentary was that of Jacobus Marthanus Pictaviensis (1539), though at least one translation circulated in manuscript and another, by Ficino, is lost (Klutstein 1987). Francesco Patrizi vastly enlarged and reorganized the corpus, which he published with his *Nova de universis philosophia* in 1591; his version incorporated a total of 320 oracles collected from Neoplatonic and patristic sources. Other translations based on the Plethonian corpus were made by Johannes Brixius (1550), Johannes Opsopaeus (1589) and Federicus Morellius (1597), while Otto Heurnius reworked Patrizi's collection to no good effect in 1600. In a letter dated ca. 1485 Janus Pannonius refers to Ficino having written a commentary on the *Oracula*, but the work is not otherwise attested and may be a confusion on Pannonius' part (Dannenfeldt 1960a).

D. Cabbala

Cabbala is a Jewish theosophical and theurgic tradition influenced by Neoplatonism and possibly by ancient Gnosticism, involving the invocation of angelic names for the sake of their supposed magical properties. All Caba-list texts properly so called are medieval in origin, and the earliest, the *Bahir*, is probably from the end of the twelfth century at the earliest. One source for the *Bahir*, the *Sefer Yetzirah*, was probably composed before the early eighth century. In the Renaissance, however, Cabalist lore was thought to go back to the time of Moses and to constitute the secret ancient theology of the Jews. Interest in Cabbala among Latin Christians first appeared in the works of Ramon Llull (ca. 1225-1315), but it was Giovanni Pico della Mirandola who was the true founder of Christian Cabalism (Wirszubski 1989). Pico employed Flavius Mithridates, a converted Sicilian Jew, to translate the Cabbala for him; this was the most ambitious project to translate Cabbalistic texts in the Ren-aissance. Mithridates' texts were never published in the Renaissance and only recently have begun to be available to scholars (Busi, Bondoni and Campanini 2004; Busi 2006). Using Mithridates' translations, Pico composed a large number of Cabbalistic theses which were included in his *900 Theses*, pub-lished in 1486. Johannes Reuchlin (1455-1522), Francesco Giorgi or Zorzi (1460-1540), Paolo Ricci (fl. 1511-1532) and Heinrich Cornelius Agrippa von Nettesheim (1487-1535) helped popularize Christian Cabalism in the sixteenth century (Benz 1958; Secret 1964). For Giordano Bruno and Cabala see Meroi 2006.

BIBLIOGRAPHY

ABBREVIATIONS

CSEL = Corpus Scriptorum Ecclesiasticorum Latinorum.

CTC = P. O. Kristeller, F. E. Cranz, and V. Brown, eds. *Catalogus Translationum et Commentariorum: Medieval and Renaissance Latin Translations and Commentaries. Annotated Lists and Guides.* 8 vols. to date. Washington, D.C. 1960-2003.

ISTC = *The Illustrated Incunabula Short-Title Catalogue on CD-ROM.* Edited by M. Davies. 2nd edition. London. 1998.

SEP = *Stanford Encyclopedia of Philosophy.* Edited by E. N. Zalta. URL: http://plato.stanford.edu

ALCINOUS 1990. *Enseignement des doctrines de Platon.* Edited by J. Whittaker. Paris.

ALLEN, M. J. B. 1994. *Nuptial Arithmetic: Marsilio Ficino's Commentary on the Fatal Number in Book VIII of Plato's Republic.* Berkeley and Los Angeles.

ALLEN, M. J. B. 1995. *Studies in Marsilio Ficino's Metaphysics and Its Sources.* Aldershot.

ALLEN, M. J. B. 1998. *Synoptic Art: Marsilio Ficino on the History of Platonic Interpretation.* Florence.

ANONYMOUS 1962. *Anonymous Prolegomenon to Platonic Philosophy*. Edited by L. G. Westerink. Amsterdam.

BARON, H. 1968. "Aulus Gellius in the Renaissance: His Influence and a Manuscript from the School of Guarino". In *From Petrarch to Leonardo Bruni: Studies in Humanistic and Political Literature*, 196-215. Chicago.

BENZ, E. 1958. *Die christliche Kabbala: Ein Stiefkind der Theologie*. Zurich.

BERTELLI, S. 1965. *La conoscenza e la diffusione di Lucrezio nei codici umanistici italiani*. Rome.

BEVAGNI, C. 1994. "Appunti sulle traduzioni latine dei *Moralia* di Plutarco nel Quattrocento". *Studi umanistici piceni* 14:71-84.

BILLANOVICH, G. 1958. *Veterum vestigia vatum. Italia medioevale e umanistica* 1:155-243.

BLACK, R., and G. POMARO 2000. *Boethius' Consolation of Philosophy in Italian Medieval and Renaissance Education: Schoolbooks and their Glosses in Florentine Manuscripts*. Florence.

BLAIR, A. 1999. "The *Problemata* as a Natural Philosophical Genre". In GRAFTON and SIRAISI 1999, 171-204.

BOSSIER, F. 1987. "Traductions latines et influences du Commentaire *In de Caelo* des Simplikios". In HADOT, I. 1987, 289-325.

BOTER, G. Forthcoming. "Epictetus". In *CTC*, vol. 9.

BOWERSOCK, G. W. 1978. *Julian the Apostate*. Cambridge, MA.

BRAMS, J., and W. VANHAMEL 1989. *Guillaume de Moerbeke: Recueil d'études à l'occasion du 700ᵉ anniversaire de sa mort 1286*. Leuven.

BRENTA, A. 1993. *In principio lectionis Aristophanis praeludia. La prolusione al corso su Aristofane*. Edited by M. A. Pincelli. Rome.

BURLEY, W. 2002. *Vida y costumbres de los viejos filósofos: la traducción castellana cuatrocentista del De vita et moribus philosophorum atribuido a Walter Burley*. Edited by F. Crosas. Madrid and Frankfurt.

BURNYEAT, M. F., ed. 1983. *The Skeptical Tradition*. Berkeley.

BUSI, G., S. M. BONDONI, and S. CAMPANINI, eds. 2004. *The Great Parchment: Flavius Mithridates' Latin translation, the Hebrew text, and an English version*. Turin.

BUSI, G., ed. 2006. *Hebrew to Latin, Latin to Hebrew: The Mirroring of Two Cultures in the Age of Humanism*. Turin.

CAMPANELLA, T. 2006. *Apologia pro Galileo*. Edited by M.-P. Lerner. Pisa.

CARDANUS, H. 1663. *Opera omnia*. Edited by C. Sponius. 10 vols. Lyons (Reprint Stuttgart-Bad Cannstatt, 1966).

CELENZA, C. 2001. *Piety and Pythagoras in Renaissance Florence: The "Symbolum Nesianum"*. Leiden and Boston.

CLÉMENT, M. 2005. *Le Cynisme à la Renaissance d'Erasme à Montaigne*. (Cahiers d'Humanisme et Renaissance, 72). Geneva.

CUTLER, I. 2006. *Cynicism from Diogenes to Dilbert*. Jefferson, NC.

CRANZ, F. E. 1960. "Alexander Aphrodisiensis". In *CTC*, 1:77-135.

CRANZ, F. E., and C. B. SCHMITT 1984. *A Bibliography of Aristotle Editions, 1501-1600*. Second edition with addenda and revisions by C. B. Schmitt. Baden-Baden.

DAMASCIUS 1959. *Lectures on the Philebus Wrongly Attributed to Olympiodorus*. Edited by L. G. Westerink. Amsterdam.

DAMASCIUS 1986-91. *Traité des premiers principes*. Edited by L. G. Westerink. Translated by J. Combès. 2 vols. Paris.

DAMASCIUS 1997. *Commentaire du Parménide de Platon*. Edited by L. G. Westerink. Translated by J. Combès. 2 vols. Paris.

DAMASCIUS, and OLYMPIODORUS 1976-77. *The Greek Commentaries on Plato's Phaedo*. Edited by L. G. Westerink. 2 vols. Amsterdam.

DANNENFELDT, K. H. 1960a. "Oracula Chaldaica". In *CTC*, 1:157-64.

DANNENFELDT, K. H. 1960b. "Hermetica Philosophica". In *CTC*, 1:137-56.

DAVIES, M. 1987. "Cosma Raimondi's *Defence of Epicurus*". *Rinascimento* n.s. 27:123-39.

DE LIBERA, A. 1984. *Introduction à la mystique rhénane: d'Albert le Grand à maître Eckhart*. Paris.

DIELS, H., ed. 1929. *Doxographi Graeci*. 2nd ed. Berlin.

DIONYSIUS THE AREOPAGITE (PSEUDO) 1937-50. *Dionysiaca: Recueil donnant l'ensemble des traductions latines des ouvrages attribués au Denys de l'Aréopage*. Edited by P. Chevalier et al. 2 vols. Paris.

DOD, B. G. 1982. "Aristoteles Latinus". In KRETZMAN ET AL. 1982, 45-79.

DOYLE, J. P. 2007. "Hispanic Scholastic Philosophy, 1526-1718". In HANKINS 2007b.

DÜRING, I. 1957. *Aristotle in the Ancient Biographical Tradition*. Göteborg.

DURLING, R. J. 1961. "A Chronological Census of Renaissance Editions and Translations of Galen". *Journal of the Warburg and Courtauld Institutes* 24:230-305.

FERGUSON, J. 1970. *Socrates: A Sourcebook*. London.

FICINO, M. 2001-06. *Platonic Theology*. Edited and translated by M. J. B. Allen and J. Hankins. 6 vols. Cambridge, MA.

FLEISCHMANN, W. B. 1971. "Lucretius Carus, Titus". In *CTC*, 2:349-65.

FLODR, M. 1973. *Incunabula classicorum. Wiegendrucke der griechischen und römischen Literatur*. Amsterdam.

FLORIDI, L. 2002. *Sextus Empiricus: The Transmission and Recovery of Pyrrhonism*. Oxford.

FLÜELER, C. 1992. *Rezeption und Interpretation der aristotelischen Politica im späten Mittelalter*. 2 vols. Amsterdam.

FOHLEN, J. 2002. "Biographie de Sénèque et commentaires des *Epistulae ad Lucilium* (V-XVᵉ siècles)". *Italia medioevale e umanistica* 43:1-90.

FREDE, M. 2006. "The early Christian reception of Socrates". In *Remembering Socrates: Philosophical Essays.* Edited by L. Judson and V. Karasmanis. Oxford.

FUBINI, R. 2002. *Humanism and Secularization: From Petrarch to Valla.* Durham, NC, and London.

GARIN, E. 1979. *La cultura filosofica del Rinascimento italiano.* 2nd ed. Florence.

GENTILE, S., ed. 1997. *L'umanesimo e padri della Chiesa: manoscritti e incunaboli di testi patristici da Francesco Petrarca al primo Cinquecento.* Exhibition catalog. Rome.

GENTILE, S., and C. GILLY, eds. 1999. *Marsilio Ficino e il ritorno di Ermete Trismegisto.* Exhibition catalog. Florence.

GERSH, S. 1986. *Middle Platonism and Neoplatonism: The Latin Tradition.* 2 vols. Notre Dame.

GIGANTE, M. 1988. "Ambrogio Traversari interprete di Diogene Laerzio". In *Ambrogio Traversari nel VI centenario della nascit*a. Convegno internazionale di studi (Camaldoli-Firenze, 15-18 settembre 1986), 367-459. Florence.

GILLY, C., and C. VAN HEERTUM, eds. 2002. *Magia, alchimia, scienza dal '400 al '700. L'influsso di Ermete Trismegisto.* Exhibition catalog. Florence.

GIUSTINIANI, V. R. 1979. "Plutarch und die humanistische Ethik". In *Ethik im Humanismus.* Edited by W. Rüegg and D. Wuttke, 45-62. Boppard.

GORDON, C. A. 1962. *A Bibliography of Lucretius.* London.

GOULET, R. 1989-2005. *Dictionnaire des philosophes antiques.* 4 vols. to date. Paris.

GRAFTON, A., and N. G. SIRAISI, eds. 1999. *Natural Particulars: Nature and the Disciplines in Renaissance Europe.* Cambridge, MA.

GRIGNASCHI, M. 1990. "Lo Pseudo-Walter Burley e il *Liber de vita et moribus philosophorum*". *Medioevo* 16:131-90. With corrigenda et addenda on pp. 325-54.

HADOT, I., ed. 1987. *Simplicius, sa vie, son oeuvre, sa survie*. Actes du Colloque Internationale (Paris, 28 septembre-1ᵉʳ octobre 1985). Berlin and New York.

HADOT, P. 1987. "La survie du Commentaire de Simplicius sur le *Manuel d'Epictète* du XVᵉ au XVIIᵉ siècles: Perotti, Politien, Steuchus, John Smith, Cudworth". In HADOT, I. 1987, 326-67.

HADZSITS, G. D. 1935. *Lucretius and His Influence*. London.

HANKINS, J. 1990. *Plato in the Italian Renaissance*. 2 vols. Leiden.

HANKINS, J. 1997. *Repertorium Brunianum. A Critical Guide to the Writings of Leonardo Bruni*. Vol. 1. (Fonti per la Storia d'Italia, Sussidi 4). Rome.

HANKINS, J. 2003-04. *Humanism and Platonism in the Italian Renaissance*. 2 vols. Rome.

HANKINS, J. 2005. "Plato's Psychogony in the Later Renaissance: Changing Attitudes to the Christianization of Pagan Philosophy". In *Platons Timaeos als Grundtext der Kosmologie in Spätantike, Mittelalter und Renaissance*. Edited by T. Leinkauf and C. Steel. (Ancient and Medieval Philosophy, 34). Leuven.

HANKINS, J. 2006. "Marsilio Ficino on *Reminiscentia* and the Transmigration of Souls". *Rinascimento* n.s. 45:3-17.

HANKINS, J. 2007a. "Socrates in the Italian Renaissance". In *Socrates, from Antiquity to the Enlightenment*. Edited by M. B. Trapp, 179-208. Aldershot.

HANKINS, J., ed. 2007b. *The Cambridge Companion to Renaissance Philosophy*. Cambridge (in press).

HANKINS, J., J. MONFASANI, and F. PURNELL JR., eds. 1987. *Supplementum Festivum: Studies in Honor of Paul Oskar Kristeller*. Binghamton, NY.

HASSE, D. N. 2007. "Arabic Philosophy and Averroism". In HANKINS 2007b.

HENINGER, S. K. 1974. *Touches of Sweet Harmony: Pythagorean Cosmology and Renaissance Poetics*. San Marino, CA.

HERMEIAS OF ALEXANDRIA 1901. *In Platonis Phaedrum scholia*. Edited by P. Couvreur. Paris.

HERMES TRISMEGISTUS (PSEUDO) 1924-36. *Hermetica. The Ancient Greek and Latin Writings which contain Religious or Philosophic Teachings Ascribed to Hermes Trismegistus*. Edited by W. Scott. 4 vols. Oxford (Reprinted Boston, 1985).

HERMES TRISMEGISTUS (PSEUDO) 1992. *Hermetica: The Greek Corpus Hermeticum and the Latin Asclepius in a New English Translation with Notes and Introduction*. Edited and translated by B. P. Copenhaver. Cambridge.

HERMIAS 1993. *Satire des philosophes païens. Irrisio gentilium philosophorum*. Edited by R. P. C. Hanson. Translated by D. Joussot. Paris.

IAMBLICHUS 1975. *De vita pythagorica liber*. Edited by L. Deubner. Stuttgart.

KLIBANSKY, R., and F. REGEN. 1993. *Die Handschriften der philosophischen Werke des Apuleius*. (Abhandlungen der Akademie der Wissenschaften in Göttingen, Philologisch-Historische Klasse, 3 Folge, Nr. 204). Göttingen.

KLUTSTEIN, I. 1987. *Marsilio Ficino et la théologie ancienne: Oracles chaldaïques, Hymnes orphiques, Hymns de Proclus*. (Quaderni di Rinascimento, 5). Florence.

KRAYE, J. 2002. *Classical Traditions in Renaissance Philosophy*. Aldershot.

KRAYE, J. 2003. "The legacy of ancient philosophy". In *The Cambridge Companion to Greek and Roman Philosophy*. Edited by D. Sedley, 323-52. Cambridge.

KRAYE, J., W. F. RYAN, and C. B. SCHMITT, eds. 1986. *Pseudo-Aristotle in the Middle Ages*. London.

KRAYE, J., and M. W. F. STONE, eds. 2000. *Humanism and Early Modern Philosophy*. London.

KRETZMANN, N., A. KENNY, and J. PINBORG with E. STUMP, eds. 1982. *The Cambridge History of Later Medieval Philosophy: From the Rediscovery of Aristotle to the Disintegration of Scholasticism, 1100-1600*. Cambridge.

KRISTELLER, P. O. 1938. *Supplementum Ficinianum*. 2 vols. Florence.

LA BRASCA, F. 1999. "Hinc mel, hinc venenum: l'édition commentée du *De rerum natura* par Giovanni Nardi (1647)". In *Présence de Lucrèce*. Edited by R. Poignault, 381-98. Tours.

LAARMANN, M. 1995. "Sokrates im Mittelalter". In *Lexikon des Mittelalters*. Edited by R. Auty et al. Vol. 7.2, s.v. Munich.

LINES, D. A. 2002a. *Aristotle's Ethics in the Italian Renaissance (ca. 1300-1650): The Universities and the Problem of Moral Education*. Leiden.

LINES, D. A. 2007. "Humanistic and Scholastic Ethics". In HANKINS 2007b.

LOHR, C. H. 1967-74. "Medieval Latin Aristotle Commentaries". *Traditio* 23 (1967):313-413, authors A-F; ibid. 24 (1968):149-245, authors G-I; ibid. 26 (1970):135-216, authors Jacobus-Johannes Juff; ibid. 27 (1971):251-351, authors Johannes de Kanthi-Myngodu; ibid. 28 (1972):281-396, authors Narcissus-Richardus; ibid. 29 (1973):93-197, authors Robertus-Wilgelmus; ibid. 30 (1974):119-44, supplement.

LOHR, C. H. 1988. *Latin Aristotle Commentaries*. II: *Renaissance Authors*. Florence.

LOHR, C. H. 2000. "Renaissance Latin Translations of the Greek Commentaries on Aristotle". In KRAYE and STONE 2000, 24-40.

LORCH, M. 1991. "The Epicurean in Lorenzo Valla's *On Pleasure*". In *Atoms, Pneuma and Tranquillity: Epicurean and Stoic Themes in European Thought*. Edited by M. J. Osler, 89-114. Cambridge.

MAHONEY, E. P., ed. 1976. *Philosophy and Humanism: Renaissance Essays in Honor of Paul Oskar Kristeller*. New York.

MAHONEY, E. P. 1982. "Neoplatonism, the Greek Commentators, and Renaissance Aristotelianism". In *Neoplatonism and Christian Thought*. Edited by D. J. O'Meara, 169-77 and 264-82. Albany.

MANETTI, G. 2003. *Biographical Writings*. Edited and translated by S. U. Baldassarri and R. Bagemihl. Cambridge, MA.

MANSFIELD, J., and D. T. RUNIA 1997. *Aëtiana: The Method and Intellectual Context of a Doxographer*. Leiden and New York.

MANSFELD 2004. "Doxography of Ancient Philosophy". In *SEP* (Summer 2004 edition).

MARINUS 1985. *Vita di Proclo*. Edited and translated by R. Masullo. Naples.

MARSH, D. 1992. "Xenophon". In *CTC*, 7:75-196.

MATTON, S. 1996. "Cynicism and Christianity from the Middle Ages to the Renaissance". In *The Cynics: The Cynic Movement in Antiquity and Its Legacy*. Edited by R. Bracht Branham and M. O. Goulet-Cazé. Berkeley and Los Angeles.

MAXIMUS OF TYRE 1997. *The Philosophical Orations*. Edited by M. B. Trapp. Oxford.

McCUAIG, W. 1989. *Carlo Sigonio. The Changing World of the Late Renaissance*. Princeton.

MEROI, F. 2006. *Cabala Parva. La filosofia di Giordano Bruno fra tradizione cristiana e pensiero moderno*. Rome.

MONFASANI, J. 1987. "Pseudo-Dionysius the Areopagite in Mid-Quatrocento Rome". In Hankins, Monfasani, and Purnell, eds. 1987, 189-214. Binghamton, NY.

MONFASANI, J. 2005. *Nicolaus Scutellius, O.S.A., as Pseudo-Pletho: The Sixteenth-Century Treatise "Pletho in Aristotelem" and the Scribe Michael Martinus Stella*. (Quaderni di Rinascimento, 41). Florence.

MORAN, D. 2007. "Nicholas of Cusa and Modern Philosophy". In HANKINS 2007b.

MUNK OLSEN, B. 1982. *L'étude des auteurs classiques latins aux XIᵉ et XIIᵉ siècles*. 3 vols. Paris.

MURRAY, A. 1986. "The Epicureans". In *Intellectuals and Writers in Four-teenth Century Europe*. Edited by P. Boitano and A. Torti, 138-63. Cambridge.

NARDI, B. 1958. *Saggi sull'aristotelismo padovano dal secolo XIV al XVI*. Florence.

NARDUCCI, E. 2004. *Cicerone e i suoi interpreti*. Pisa.

NESCHKE-HENTSCHKE, A., ed. 2000. *Le Timée de Platon: Contributions à l'histoire de sa réception*. (Bibliothèque philosophique de Louvain, 53). Louvain.

NESCHKE-HENTSCHKE, A., ed. 1995-2003. *Platonisme politique et théorie du droit naturel: Contributions à une archéologie de la culture politique européene*. 3 vols. (Bibliothèque philosophique de Louvain, 42, 61). Louvain.

OLDFATHER, W. A. 1927. *Contributions Toward a Bibliography of Epictetus*. Urbana.

OLIVER, R. P. 1954. *Niccolò Perotti's version of the Enchiridion of Epictetus*. Urbana.

O'MEARA, D. 1992. "Plotinus". In *CTC*, 7:55-74.

PAGNONI, M. R. 1974. "Prime note sulla tradizione medioevale ed umanistica di Epicuro". *Annali della Scuola Normale Superiore di Pisa*, s. 3, 4:1143-77.

PANAETIUS 1952. *Fragmenta*. Edited by M. Van Straaten. Leiden.

PANIZZA, L. A. 1977. "Gasparino Barzizza's Commentaries on Seneca's *Letters*". *Traditio* 33:297-358.

PAQUET, L. 1988. *Les Cyniques grecs: fragments et témoignages*. 2nd ed. Ottawa.

PERFETTI, S. 2000. *Aristotle's Zoology and its Renaissance Commentators (1521-1601)*. Leuven.

PHILOPONUS (PSEUDO) 1991. *Pseudo-Johannis Philoponi Expositiones in omnes XIV Aristotelis Libros metaphysicos*. Stuttgart-Bad Cannstatt.

PHILOSTRATUS 2005. *The Life of Apollonius of Tyana*. Translated by C. P. Jones. 3 vols. (The Loeb Classical Library, 16-17). Cambridge, MA.

PHILOSTRATUS 2006. *Apollonius of Tyana: Letters of Apollonius, ancient testimonia, Eusebius' reply to Hierocles*. Translated by C. P. Jones (The Loeb Classical Library, 458). Cambridge, MA.

PIZZANI, U. 1986. "Dimensione cristiana dell'Umanesimo e messaggio lucreziano: la *Paraphrasis in Lucretium* di Raphael Francus". In *Validità perenne dell'Umanesimo. Atti del XXV e XXVI Convegno Internazionale di Studi Umanistici*. Florence.

PLETHO 1995. *Oracles chaldaïques, recension de Georges Gémiste Pléthon*. Edited and translated by B. Tambrun-Krasker. Athens and Paris.

PORPHYRY 1993. *Fragmenta*. Edited by A. Smith. Stuttgart and Leipzig.

POSIDONIUS 1989. *Selections*. Vol. 1. Edited by L. Edelstein and I. G. Kidd. 2nd ed. Cambridge (1st edition, 3 vols, 1972).

PROCLUS 1899. *Procli Diadochi in Platonis Rem publicam commentarii*. Edited by W. Kroll. Leipzig.

PROCLUS 1900-03. *Commentaire sur le Parménide, suivi du commentaire anonyme sur le VII dernières hypothèses*. Translated by A.-E. Chaignet. Paris.

PROCLUS 1903. *In Platonis Timaeum commentaria*. Edited by E. Diehl. Leipzig.

PROCLUS 1908. *In Platonis Cratylum commentaria*. Edited by G. Pasquali. Leipzig.

PROCLUS 1982-85. *Proclus: Commentaire sur le Parmènide de Platon. Traduction de Guillaume de Moerbeke*. Edited by C. Steel. 2 vols. Leuven.

PROCLUS 1985-86. *Sur le premier Alcibiade de Platon*. Edited by A. Ph. Segonds. 2 vols. Paris.

PROSPERI, V. 2004. *Di soavi licor gli orli del vaso: La fortuna di Lucrezio dall'Umanesimo alla Controriforma*. Turin.

REEVE, M. D. 1980. "The Italian Tradition of Lucretius". *Italia medioevale e umanistica* 23:27-46.

REYNOLDS, L. D. 1965. *The Medieval Tradition of Seneca's "Letters"*. Oxford.

REYNOLDS, L. D., ed., 1983. *Texts and Transmission: A Survey of the Latin Classics*. Oxford.

RIGINOS, A. S. 1976. *Platonica: The Anecdotes Concerning the Life and Writings of Plato*. Leiden.

RISSE, W. 1998. *Bibliographia philosophica vetus. Repertorium generale systematicum operum philosophicorum usque ad annum MDCCC typis impressorum*. 9 parts. Hildesheim.

RUNIA, D. T. 1999. "What is Doxography?" In *Ancient Histories of Medicine: Essays in Medical Doxography and Historiography in Classical Antiquity*, 33-55. Edited by P. J. van der Eijk. Leiden.

SALLUSTIUS 1960. *De diis et mundo. Des dieux et du monde*. Edited by G. Rochefort. Paris.

SCHMITT, C. B. 1971a. "Olympiodorus". In *CTC*, 2:199-204.

SCHMITT, C. B. 1971b. "Theophrastus". In *CTC*, 2:239-322.

SCHMITT, C. B. 1983a. *Aristotle and the Renaissance*. Cambridge, MA.

SCHMITT, C. B. 1983b. "The Rediscovery of Ancient Skepticism in Modern Times". In BURNYEAT 1983.

SCHMITT, C. B. 1989. *Reappraisals in Renaissance Thought*. Edited by C. Webster. London.

SCHMITT, C. B., and D. KNOX 1985. *Pseudo-Aristoteles Latinus: A Guide to Latin Works Falsely Attributed to Aristotle before 1500*. London.

SCHMITT, C. B., Q. SKINNER, and E. KESSLER with J. KRAYE, eds. 1988. *The Cambridge History of Renaissance Philosophy*. Cambridge.

SCHOLTEN, C. 1996. *Antike Naturphilosophie und christliche Kosmologie in der Schrift "De opificio mundi" des Johannes Philoponos*. Berlin.

SECRET, F. 1964. *Les Kabbalistes chretiens de la Renaissance*. Paris.

SOLARO, G. 2000. *Lucrezio: Biografie umanistiche*. Bari.

SORABJI, R., ed. 1990. *Aristotle Transformed. The Ancient Commentators and Their Influence*. London.

SOUDEK, J. 1968. "Leonardo Bruni and his Public: a Statistical and Interpretative Study of his Annotated Latin Version of the Pseudo-Aristotelian *Economics*". *Studies in Medieval and Renaissance History* 5:49-136.

SOUDEK, J. 1976. "A Fifteenth-Century Humanistic Best-seller: the Manuscript Diffusion of Leonardo Bruni's Annotated Latin Version of the Pseudo-Aristotelian *Economics*". In MAHONEY 1976, 129-143.

TAMBRUN, B. 2006. *Pléthon: Le Retour de Platon*. Paris.

THESLEFF, H., ed. 1965. *The Pythagorean Texts of the Hellenistic Period*. Åbo.

THIJSSEN, J. M. M. H., and H. A. G. BRAAKHUIS 1999. *The Commentary Tradition on Aristotle's De generatione et corruptione: Ancient, Medieval and Early Modern*. Turnhout.

TIGERSTEDT, E. N. 1974. *The Decline and Fall of the Neoplatonic Interpretation of Plato: An Outline and Some Observations*. Helsinki.

TODD, R. B. 2003. "Themistius". In *CTC*, 8:57-102.

TRAPP, M. B. 1997-8. "Zanobi Acciaiuoli, Laurentianus Conventi Soppressi 4, and the text of Maximus of Tyre". *Bulletin of the Institute of Classical Studies* 42:159-81.

TRINKAUS, C. 1983. "Humanism and Greek Sophism: Protagoras in the Renaissance". In C. Trinkaus, *The Scope of Renaissance Humanism*, 169-91. Ann Arbor.

VERBEKE, G. 1983. *The Presence of Stoicism in Medieval Thought*. Washington, D.C.

VON ARNIM, J. 1903-24. *Stoicorum veterum fragmenta*. 4 vols. Leipzig.

VON MOOSBURG, B. 1974-84. *Expositio super Elementationem theologicam Procli*. Edited by M. R. Pagnoni Sturlese and L. Sturlese. 2 vols. Hamburg.

WHITTAKER, J. 1973. "Varia Procliana". *Greek, Roman and Byzantine Studies* 14.4:427-28.

WIRSZUBSKI, C. 1989. *Pico della Mirandola's Encounter with Jewish Mysticism*. Cambridge, MA.

WORSTBRUCK, F. J. 1976. *Deutsche Antikerezeption, 1450-1550*. Boppard am Rhein.

INDEX OF NAMES[*]

---

[*] Numbers given in bold indicate the main entry for a given figure.

TIBERGRAPH

CITTÀ DI CASTELLO • PG

FINITO DI STAMPARE NEL MESE DI FEBBRAIO 2008

ISTITUTO NAZIONALE DI STUDI SUL RINASCIMENTO

PUBBLICAZIONI

ARDITI, B., *Diario di Firenze e di altre parti della cristianità (1574-1579)*. 1970. XXX-246 pp.

CAMMELLI, G., *I dotti bizantini e le origini dell'Umanesimo. III: Demetrio Calcondila*. 1954. 154 pp. con 5 tavv. f.t.

CAMPOREALE, S.I., *Lorenzo Valla. Umanesimo e teologia*. 1972. X-554 pp.

CARO, A., *Lettere familiari*. Vol. I. 1957. Vol. II. 1959. Vol. III. 1961. XXVI-1070 pp. complessive con 4 tavv. f.t.

FATINI, G., *Bibliografia della critica ariostea (1510-1956)*. 1958. XVI-726 pp.

Francesco Guicciardini nel IV Centenario della morte (1540-1940). 1940. 304 pp. con 7 ill. n.t. e 21 tavv. f.t.

LOMAZZO, G.P., *Idea del tempio della pittura*. A cura di R. Klein. 1974. 2 voll. di IV-792.

MEDICI (DE'), G. (Duca di Nemours), *Poesie*. A cura di G. Fatini. 1939. Esaurito.

NARDI, B., *Studi su Pietro Pomponazzi*. 1965. X-404 con 1 tav. f.t.

PATRIZI DA CHERSO, F., *Della Poetica*. A cura di D. Aguzzi Barbagli. Vol. I. 1969. Vol. II. 1970. Vol. III. 1971. XXII-1308 pp. complessive.

— *L'amorosa filosofia*. A cura di J.C. Nelson. 1963. XVI-150.

— *Lettere e opuscoli inediti*. A cura di D. Aguzzi Barbagli. 1975. XXIV-570 pp.

PONTANI IOANNIS IOVIANI, *De Magnanimitate*. A cura di F. Tateo. 1969. XLII-132 pp.

RICCI, P.G. - RUBINSTEIN, N., *Censimento delle lettere di Lorenzo di Piero de' Medici*. 1964. XII-200 pp.

STÄUBLE, A., *La commedia umanistica del Quattrocento*. 1968. Esaurito.

VERDE, A.F., *Lo Studio Fiorentino (1473-1503). Ricerche e documenti*. 1973. XII-396 pp.

— — *Docenti, dottorati*. 1973. IV-784 con 1 ill. f.t.

— — *Studenti, «fanciulli a scuola» nel 1480*. 1977. 2 tomi di LII-1210 pp.

— — *La vita universitaria*. 1985. 3 tomi di LVIII-1548 pp. con 6 tavv. f.t.

— — *Gli stanziamenti*. 1994. XIV-598 pp.

— — *Indici*. In preparazione.

VESPASIANO DA BISTICCI. *Le Vite*. A cura di A. Greco. Vol. I. 1970. Vol. II, 1976. LXVI-1334 pp.

ATTI DI CONVEGNI

1. *Atti del secondo Convegno Nazionale di Studi sul Rinascimento*. 1940. Esaurito.

2. *Studi vasariani*. 1952. Esaurito.

3. *Il Rinascimento: significato e limiti*. 1953. Esaurito.

4. *Il Poliziano e il suo tempo*. 1957. Esaurito.

5. *Il mondo antico nel Rinascimento*. 1958. Esaurito.

6. *Arte, pensiero e cultura a Mantova nel primo Rinascimento in rapporto con la Toscana e con il Veneto*. 1965. Esaurito.

7. *L'opera e il pensiero di Giovanni Pico della Mirandola nella storia dell'Umanesimo*. 1965. 2 voll. di XXIV-714 con 14 tavv. f.t.

8. *Donatello e il suo tempo*. 1968. XVIII-408 pp. con 92 tavv. f.t.

9. *Il pensiero politico di Machiavelli e la sua fortuna nel mondo*. 1972. X-172 pp.

10. *Movimenti ereticali in Italia e in Polonia nei secoli XVI-XVII*. 1974. 286 pp.

11. *Il Vasari storiografo e artista*. 1976. XX-876 pp. con 158 ill.

12. *Lorenzo Ghiberti nel suo tempo*. 1980. 2 voll. di XII-670 pp. con 204 ill. n.t.

13. *Il tumulto dei Ciompi. Un momento di storia fiorentina ed europea*. 1981. XXII-282 pp.

14. *Scienze, credenze occulte, livelli di cultura*. 1982. VI-564 pp. con 6 tavv. f.t.

15. *Giorgio Vasari tra decorazione ambientale e storiografia artistica*. A cura di G.C. Garfagnini. 1985. VI-426 pp. con 94 ill. f.t.

16. *Callimaco Esperiente poeta e politico del '400*. A cura di G.C. Garfagnini. 1987. XII-320 pp.

17. *Ambrogio Traversari nel VI centenario della nascita*. A cura di G.C. Garfagnini. 1988. VIII-544 pp. con 11 tavv. f.t.

18. *Leonardo Bruni cancelliere della Repubblica di Firenze*. A cura di P. Viti. 1990. XVIII-429 pp. con 10 tavv. f.t.

19. *Lorenzo il Magnifico e il suo mondo*. A cura di G.C. Garfagnini. 1994. XX-470 pp. con 43 tavv. f.t.

20. *Giordano Bruno, 1583-1585. The English Experience / L'esperienza inglese*. A cura di M. Ciliberto e N. Mann. 1997. X-182 pp.

21. *Immagini per conoscere. Dal Rinascimento alla rivoluzione scientifica*. A cura di F. Meroi e C.

Pogliano. 2001. XII-134 pp. con 65 figg. n.t. e 21 figg. f.t.

22. *I Medici in rete. Ricerca e progettualità scientifica a proposito dell'archivio* Mediceo avanti il Principato. A cura di I. Cotta e F. Klein. 2003. XIV-276 pp.

23. *La magia nell'Europa moderna. Tra antica sapienza e filosofia naturale.* A cura di F. Meroi, con la collaborazione di E. Scapparone. 2007. 2 tomi di complessive XII-786 pp. con 4 tavv. f.t..

24. *Il ritratto nell'Europa del Cinquecento.* A cura di A. Galli, C. Piccinini e M. Rossi. 2007. VIII-302 pp. con 45 tavv. f.t. di cui 1 a colori.

25. *Forme del neoplatonismo. Dall'eredità ficiniana ai platonici di Cambridge.* A cura di L. Simonutti. 2007. X-560 pp. con 4 figg. n.t. e 4 tavv. f.t.

CARTEGGI UMANISTICI

1. BRACCIOLINI, P., *Lettere.* A cura di H. Harth. Vol. I. *Lettere a Niccolò Niccoli.* 1984. CXXVI-256 pp.

2. — Vol. II. *Epistolarum familiarium libri.* 1984. XII-478 pp.

3. — Vol. III. *Epistolarum familiarium libri secundum volumen.* 1987. XII-580.

4. FICINO, M., *Lettere.* A cura di S. Gentile. Vol. I. *Epistolarum familiarium liber I.* 1990. CCC-324 pp. Rilegato.

5. BARBARO, F., *Epistolario.* A cura di C. Griggio. Vol. I. *La tradizione manoscritta e a stampa.* 1991. VIII-412 pp. con 5 tavv. f.t. Rilegato.

6. BARBARO, F., *Epistolario.* Vol. II. *La raccolta canonica delle «Epistole».* 1999. LIV-812 pp. Rilegato.

QUADERNI DI «RINASCIMENTO»

1. ALBERTI, L.B., *Intercenali inedite.* 1965. Esaurito.

2. MARTELLI, M., *L'altro Niccolò di Bernardo Machiavelli.* 1975. 62 pp.

3. FIORAVANTI, G., *Università e città. Cultura umanistica e cultura scolastica a Siena nel '400.* 1981. Esaurito

4. PARENTI, G., *Poëta Proteus alter. Forma e storia di tre libri di Pontano.* 1985. IV-148 pp.

5. KLUTSTEIN, I., *Marsilio Ficino et la théologie ancienne. Oracles chaldaïques, hymnes orphiques, hymnes de Proclus.* 1987. 128 pp.

6. STURLESE, R., *Bibliografia, censimento e storia delle antiche stampe di Giordano Bruno.* 1987. XLVIII-228 pp. con 16 tavv. f.t.

7. KRISTELLER, P.O., *Marsilio Ficino and His Work After Five Hundred Years.* 1987. VI-230 con 17 tavv. f.t.

8. REDDITI, F., *Exhortatio ad Petrum Medicem.* A cura di P. Viti. 1989. LVI-154 pp.

9. ERIZZO, S., *Lettera sulla poesia.* A cura di S. Zoppi. 1989. IV-80 pp.

10. *Bartolommeo Cederni and his friends. Letters to an obscure Florentine.* Essay by F.W. Kent. Texts edited by G. Corti e F.W. Kent. 1991. VI-128 pp.

11. NICOLÒ, A., *Il carteggio di Cassiano dal Pozzo. Catalogo.* 1991. XII-324 pp.

12. FABBRI, L., *Alleanza matrimoniale e patriziato nella Firenze del '400. Studio sulla famiglia Strozzi.* 1991. XVIII-240 pp. con 4 tavv. f.t. e 1 pieghevole.

13. AVERROÈ, *Parafrasi della «Repubblica» nella traduzione latina di Elia del Medigo.* A cura di A. Coviello e P.E. Fornaciari. 1992. XXVI-134 pp.

14. MATUCCI, A., *Machiavelli nella storiografia fiorentina. Per la storia di un genere letterario.* 1991. 278 pp.

15. *Lorenzo il Magnifico e il suo tempo.* A cura di G.C. Garfagnini. 1992. X-176 pp.

16. PATRIZI DA CHERSO, F., *«Nova de universis philosophia». Materiali per un'edizione emendata.* A cura di A.L. Puliafito Bluel. 1993. LXII-108 pp.

17. *La biblioteca dell'Istituto. Fondi speciali.* 1992. II-166 pp.

18. PARENTI, G., *Benet Garret detto il Cariteo. Profilo di un poeta.* 1993. IV-166 pp.

19. MALQUORI, A., *'Tempo d'aversità'. Gli affreschi dell'altana di Palazzo Rucellai.* 1993. IV-112 pp. con 32 tavv. f.t.

20. *La Biblioteca dell'Istituto. Catalogo dei microfilms.* A cura di G.M. Cao. 1995. VI-106 pp.

21. YOHANAN, A., *Hay ha-'olamim (L'immortale).* A cura di F. Lelli. Parte I: *La retorica.* 1995. VI-188 pp. con 4 ill. f.t.

22. ECKSTEIN, N.A., *The District of the Green Dragon. Neighbourhood life and social change in Renaissance Florence.* 1995. XXVI-276 pp. con 7 tavv. f.t.

23. CAREW-REID, N., *Les fêtes florentines au temps de Lorenzo il Magnifico.* 1995. X-292 pp.

24. PROCACCI, U., *Studi sul catasto fiorentino.* 1996. XII-190 pp.

25. HUNT, J., *Politian and Scholastic Logic. An unknown Dialogue by a Dominican Friar.* 1995. VI-234 pp.

26. ANGELO DA VALLOMBROSA, *Lettere.* A cura di L. Lunetta. 1997. XXX-124 pp.

27. CIAPPELLI, G., *Una famiglia e le sue ricordanze. I Castellani di Firenze nel Tre-Quattrocento.* 1995. VI-252 pp. con 4 ill. f.t.

28. HOWARD, P.F., *Beyond the Written Word. Preaching and Theology in the Florence of Archbishop Antoninus, 1427-1459.* 1995. XII-294 pp.

29. DE' ROSSI, G., *Vita di Federico da Montefeltro.* A cura di V. Bramanti. 1995. LVI-98 pp.

30. GREEN, L., *Lucca under Many Masters. A Fourteenth-Century Italian Commune in Crisis (1328-1342).* 1995. X-364 pp.

31. PERUZZI, E., *La nave di Ermete. La cosmologia di Girolamo Fracastoro.* 1995. VIII-120 pp.

32. JAMES, C., *Giovanni Sabadino degli Arienti. A literary career.* 1996. VIII-162 pp.

33. COMANDUCCI, R.M., *Il carteggio di Bernardo Rucellai. Inventario.* 1996. XLVIII-114 pp.

34. MUCCILLO, M., *Platonismo, ermetismo e «Prisca theologia». Ricerche di storiografia filosofica rinascimentale.* 1996. XIV-310 pp.

35. *La biblioteca dell'Istituto Nazionale di Studi sul Rinascimento. Carte Poggi.* A cura di R. Tampieri. 1997. XII-398 pp.

36. ZAGGIA, M. - MULAS, P. L. - CERIANA, M., *Giovanni Matteo Bottigella cortigiano, uomo di lettere e committente d'arte.* 1997. VIII-354 pp. con 24 ill. f.t.

37. *La biblioteca dell'Istituto Nazionale di Studi sul Rinascimento. Estratti.* A cura di L. Lanza. 1997. VI-246 pp.

38. *Indice dei nomi, dei luoghi e delle cose notevoli nelle opere latine di Giordano Bruno.* A cura di C. Lefons. 1998. 72 pp.

39. BACCHELLI, F., *Giovanni Pico e Pier Leone da Spoleto. Tra filosofia dell'amore e tradizione cabalistica.* 2001. VIII-158 pp.

40. DE BELLIS, E., *Bibliografia di Agostino Nifo.* 2005. X-290 pp.

41. JOHN MONFASANI, *Nicolaus Scutellius, O.S.A., as Pseudo-Pletho. The Sixteenth-Century Treatise Pletho in Aristotelem and the Scribe Michael Martinus Stella.* 2005. X-182 pp. con 7 tavv. f.t.

42. *Della tirannia: Machiavelli con Bartolo.* A cura di J. Barthas. 2007. XIV-116 pp.

43. *Per Giuseppe Billanovich.* A cura di M. Cortesi. 2007. VIII-66 pp.

44. HANKINS, J. - PALMER, A., *The Recovery of Ancient Philosophy in the Renaissance: A Brief Guide.* 2008. VIII-96 pp.

STUDI E TESTI

1. VALLA, L., *Collatio Novi Testamenti.* A cura di A. Perosa. 1970. LVIII-306 pp. con 4 tavv. f.t.

2. POLIZIANO, A., *Commento inedito all'epistola ovidiana di Saffo a Faone.* A cura di E. Lazzeri. 1971. XVIII-114 con 2 tavv. f.t.

3. — *La commedia antica e l'«Andria» di Terenzio.* A cura di R. Lattanzi Roselli. 1973. Esaurito.

4. CARDINI, R., *La critica del Landino.* 1973. 396 pp.

5. POLIZIANO, A., *Commento inedito alle «Selve» di Stazio.* A cura di L. Cesarini Martinelli. 1978. XXVI-794 pp. con 3 tavv. f.t.

6. LANDINO, C., *Disputationes Camaldulenses.* A cura di P. Lohe. 1980. Esaurito.

7. PALMIERI, M., *Vita civile.* A cura di G. Belloni. 1982. Esaurito.

8. *Poggio Bracciolini (1380-1980) nel VI centenario della nascita.* 1982. VIII-360 pp.

9. *Francesco Guicciardini (1483-1983) nel V centenario della nascita.* 1983. VIII-302 pp.

10. SALUTATI, C., *De fato et fortuna.* A cura di C. Bianca. 1985. CXLIV-256 pp.

11. POLIZIANO, A., *Commento inedito alle «Satire» di Persio.* A cura di L. Cesarini Martinelli e R. Ricciardi. 1985. LXXVI-164 pp.

12. MEDICI (DE'), L., *Stanze.* A cura di R. Castagnola. 1986. C-96 pp.

13. VIOLI, L., *Le giornate.* A cura di G.C. Garfagnini. 1986. LXX-430 pp. con 4 tavv. f.t.

14. *Alle bocche della piazza. Diario di anonimo fiorentino (1382-1401).* A cura di A. Mohlo e F. Sznura. 1986. LVI-252 pp. con 1 tav. f.t.

15. *Marsilio Ficino e il ritorno di Platone.* A cura di G.C. Garfagnini. 1986. 2 tomi di X-720 pp. con 20 tavv. f.t.

16. FICINO, M., *El libro dell'amore.* A cura di S. Niccoli. 1987. LX-234 pp.

17. SANNAZARO, I., *De partu Virginis.* A cura di C. Fantazzi e A. Perosa. 1988. CXXVI-134 pp. con 5 tavv. f.t.

18. POLIZIANO, A., *Commento inedito alle Georgiche di Virgilio.* A cura di L. Castano Musicò. 1990. XVI-282 pp.

19. *I Guicciardini e le scienze occulte.* A cura di R. Castagnola. 1990. VIII-400 con 8 tavv. f.t.

20. MARKOWSKI, M., *Astronomica et astrologica Cracoviensia ante annum 1550.* 1990. XXVI-380 pp.

21. MEDICI (DE'), L., *Laude.* A cura di B. Toscani. 1990. VI-124 pp.

22. DALLE CELLE, G. - MARSILI, L., *Lettere.* A cura di F. Giambonini. 1991. 2 tomi di X-606 pp.

23. POLIZIANO, A., *Commento inedito ai «Fasti» di Ovidio.* A cura di F. Lo Monaco. 1991. XXXVIII-554 pp. con 1 tav. f.t.

24. MEDICI (DE'), L., *Canzoniere.* A cura di T. Zanato. 1991. 2 tomi di XX-608 con 2 tavv. f.t.

25. — *Comento de' miei sonetti.* A cura di T. Zanato. 1991. VIII-344 pp.

26. BRUNO, G., *De umbris idearum.* A cura di R. Sturlese. 1991. LXXXIV-250 con 4 tavv. f.t. e molte ill. n.t.

27. *Lorenzo de' Medici. Studi.* A cura di G.C. Garfagnini. 1992. XIV-356 pp.

28. CASTELLANI, F., *Ricordanze. I: Ricordanze «A» (1436-1459).* A cura di G. Ciappelli. 1992. X-214 con 2 tavv. f.t.

29. CERRETANI, B., *Ricordi.* A cura di G. Berti. 1993. XIV-480 pp.

30. — *Dialogo della mutatione di Firenze.* A cura di G. Berti. 1993. VI-100 pp.

31. — *Storia fiorentina.* A cura di G. Berti. 1994. XX-476 pp.

32. TORNABUONI, L., *Lettere.* A cura di P. Salvadori. 1993. VIII-216 pp.

33. PARENTI, P., *Storia fiorentina. I (1476-78 ~ 1492-96).* A cura di A. Matucci. 1994. LII-366 pp.

34. BULLARD, M.M., *Lorenzo il Magnifico. Image, anxiety, politics and finance.* 1994. XVI-248 pp.

35. BRUNI, L., *Dialogi ad Petrum Paulum Histrum.* A cura di S.U. Baldassarri. 1994. XXII-308 pp.

36. CASTELLANI, F., *Ricordanze. II: Quaternuccio e Giornale B (1459-1485).* A cura di G. Ciappelli. 1995. VIII-270 pp. con 4 tavv. f.t.

37. NEWBIGIN, N., *Feste d'Oltrarno. Plays in churches in Fifteenth-century Florence.* 1996. 2 tomi di XVI-796 pp. con 5 tavv. f.t.

38. PARENTI, M., *Lettere.* A cura di M. Marrese. 1996. XXXIV-272 pp.

39. POLIZIANO, A., *Silvae.* A cura di F. Bausi. 1997. LIV-404 pp.

40. ALLEN, M.J.B., *Synoptic Art. Marsilio Ficino on the History of platonic Interpretation.* 1998. XIV-236 pp.

41. MICHELE CILIBERTO - NICOLETTA TIRINNANZI, *Il dialogo recitato. Per una nuova edizione del Bruno volgare.* 2002. XII-174 pp.

42. *Humanistica. Per Cesare Vasoli.* A cura di F. Meroi e E. Scapparone. 2004. VIII-404 pp.

43. *La mente di Giordano Bruno.* A cura di F. Meroi, con saggio introduttivo di M. Ciliberto. 2004. XXXVI-592 pp.

44. SIMONETTA BASSI, *L'arte di Giordano Bruno. Memoria, furore, magia.* 2004. XIV-240 pp.

45. PIETRO POMPONAZZI, *Expositio super primo et secundo De partibus animalium.* A cura di S. Perfetti. 2004. LXXXVI-362 pp. con 2 tavv. f.t.

46. PARENTI, P., *Storia fiorentina. II (1496-1502).* A cura di A. Matucci. 2005. VIII-550 pp.

47. BARTOLUCCI, G., *La repubblica ebraica di Carlo Sigonio. Modelli politici dell'età moderna.* 2007. X-216 pp.

TEATRO LATINO DEL RINASCIMENTO

1. BRUNI, L., *Versione del «Pluto» di Aristofane.* A cura di E. e M. Cecchini. 1965. XXXIV-22 pp.

2. PICCOLOMINI, E.S., *Chrysis.* A cura di E. Cecchini. 1968. XXVI-46 pp.

* * *

«La Rinascita»
Rivista del Centro (poi Istituto) Nazionale di Studi sul Rinascimento
Diretta da Giovanni Papini
Collezione completa. *I-VII, 1938-1944, nn. 1-35.*

«Rinascimento», Rivista dell'Istituto Nazionale di Studi sul Rinascimento.
Annuale, seconda serie diretta da Michele Ciliberto e Cesare Vasoli. Fondata nel 1950.
I serie: I-XI, 1950-1960; *II serie*: I, 1961-

SUPPLEMENTI
*«La Rinascita» (1938-1944), «Rinascimento» (1950-1983). Indici sommari (Autori, Recensioni,
Notizie, Documenti, Personaggi e argomenti).* A cura di Gian Carlo Garfagnini
1985, x-114 pp., suppl. a «Rinascimento», vol. XXIV

Bibliografia italiana di studi sull'Umanesimo ed il Rinascimento.
A cura di L. Boschetto e G.M. Cao
1985-88, suppl. a «Rinascimento», voll. XXVI-XXIX

CASA EDITRICE LEO S. OLSCHKI